Daily Ir

Another book to
add to your life) ! :)
Hope you enjoy it ..

Love you — ♡
your babe
sister sister

Other Books by These Authors

Ginny Kubitz Moyer

Random MOMents of Grace

Mary and Me

Jessica Mesman Griffith

Love & Salt

Vinita Hampton Wright

The Art of Spiritual Writing

Praying Freedom

Days of Deepening Friendship

Simple Acts of Moving Forward

The St. Thérèse of Lisieux Prayer Book

Margaret Silf

Just Call Me López

Simple Faith

The Other Side of Chaos

Inner Compass

Compass Points

Daily Inspiration for Women
Seasons of a Woman's Life

Spring + Summer + Autumn + Winter

GINNY KUBITZ MOYER

JESSICA MESMAN GRIFFITH

VINITA HAMPTON WRIGHT

MARGARET SILF

LOYOLA PRESS.
A JESUIT MINISTRY

Chicago

LOYOLA PRESS.
A JESUIT MINISTRY

3441 N. Ashland Avenue
Chicago, Illinois 60657
(800) 621-1008
www.loyolapress.com

"The Peace of Wild Things" from *New Collected Poems* by Wendell Berry.
Copyright © 2012 Wendell Berry. Used by permission of Counterpoint.

"The Grasses" and "Who Makes These Changes?" are from *The Essential Rumi*.
Copyright © 1995 by Coleman Barks. Permission granted by Coleman Barks.

Unless otherwise indicated all Scripture quotations contained herein are from the
New Revised Standard Version Bible: Catholic Edition, copyright © 1993 and 1989
by the Division of Christian Education of the National Council of the Churches of
Christ in the U.S.A. Used by permission. All rights reserved.

Scripture passages cited as *New Jerusalem Bible* translation are taken from *The New
Jerusalem Bible* © 1985 by Darton, Longman & Todd Ltd and Doubleday, a
division of Bantam Doubleday Dell Publishing Group, Inc.

Scripture passages cited as *New International Version* translation are taken from
Holy Bible, New International Version®. Copyright © 1973, 1978, 1984 by
International Bible Society. Used by permission of Zondervan Publishing House.
All rights reserved.

The "NIV" and "New International Version" trademarks are registered in the
United States Patent and Trademark Office by the International Bible Society. Use
of either trademark requires the permission of the International Bible Society.

Cover art credit: From top to bottom, ©iStockphoto.com/Ale-ks,
©iStockphoto.com/belchonock, ©iStockphoto.com/small_frog,
©iStockphoto.com/wrangel.

ISBN-13: 978-0-8294-4041-6
ISBN-10: 0-8294-4041-0
Library of Congress Control Number: 2013950592

Printed in the United States of America.

13 14 15 16 17 18 Bang 10 9 8 7 6 5 4 3 2 1

Contents

Introduction

Women keep buying devotional books because devotional books meet a specific kind of need. Often we are too busy to dip into a book for thirty minutes to start our day. We are driving kids to school, going to work, caring for elderly parents or grandparents, doing creative work inside and outside the home, and managing multiple projects. We need a few well-placed words that meet us where we live. We are hungry for wisdom and encouragement, but we'd rather not have to do all the searching ourselves.

We also don't need light, feel-good readings that don't really urge us to reflect and tackle our lives with courage and integrity. We need help with our anxiety, frustration, anger, and desire. We want honest, searching words that might sting but that will help us move forward.

Here's another thing: our lives don't unfold according to a calendar year. We live day by day, but we also live by seasons. Not surprisingly, a woman's seasons often reflect the physical, cyclical seasons of the earth. We are intimately acquainted with the birthing and open-endedness that is spring, the blooming and high activity that is summer, the relinquishment and slowing down that is autumn, and the dormant difficult growth—and quiet recollection—called winter.

So this woman's book of inspiration is organized by seasons, beginning in spring and ending in winter. It does not start in January—but you, reader, may start wherever you want. This is a page-a-day book, but the choice of day is entirely up to you. You don't have to begin or end at a certain time and on a certain page.

An added bonus of this material is the careful selection of authors. Four women have offered their gifts to you—each woman took a season and unfolded her wisdom around it. Spring and Summer come to us from Ginny Kubitz Moyer and Jessica Mesman Griffith, both working moms and gifted writers. Autumn writings are by me—Vinita Wright, a spirituality writer/editor in my fifties. And Winter issues from the profound and loving insight of Margaret Silf, who technically is a senior (also a mom and grandma) but whose extensive retreat work spans the globe.

So, you grasp in your hands (whether print book or e-book) the collective wisdom and wonder of writers chosen especially for this task. Not only have we written from the truth of our own lives, but also we have gleaned our favorite quotes from writers, teachers, saints, and mystics.

Use this book as your needs require. Start anywhere, linger where you need to linger, dwell with joy and intention in your particular season of life—but taste often and deeply of the other seasons, too.

Vinita Hampton Wright

Spring

Ginny Kubitz Moyer

In some places, spring arrives quickly. Flowers burst into bloom, and by early April it's warm enough for sandals and shorts.

In other places, spring comes slowly, playing a tantalizing game of hide-and-seek between storms and snow.

However it arrives, spring is always something to celebrate. The cold of winter has relaxed its grip, and the warmth invites us to venture out of our homes and savor the new life we glimpse in flowerbeds and tree branches and fields.

Are you feeling eager for a fresh beginning? Spring offers that in abundance. It's a period of possibility, God's gentle reminder that there will always be another chance to make a new start.

SPRING

March 1

It is always spring in the soul united to God.
—St. John Vianney

What does it mean to be united to God?

There are plenty of days when a layer of something—lethargy, despair, stress—makes me feel distant from God. But just as spring always follows winter, I have found that if I give it time and pray, that barrier always melts away, like frost on a field when the sun comes up. There is a gradual thaw, and I am once again able to feel the warmth of the creator God, a presence that has been there all along.

When have you felt particularly close to God? Relive that experience in God's presence, knowing that God takes as much joy in it as you do.

March 2

Who has seen the wind?
Neither I nor you;
But when the leaves hang trembling,
The wind is passing through.
—Christina Rossetti, "Who Has Seen the Wind?"

In the San Francisco Bay area, we get a lot of stiff breezes. The wind is unseen but so constant, so strong, that it has a presence you don't often forget. It ruffles my hair, scatters papers and leaves, and—if I'm particularly mindful—makes me think of the Holy Spirit.

In the same way, we don't *see* the Spirit, but evidence of the Spirit rustles through so many of our encounters with others. Anytime we see acts of charity, faith, zeal, and wisdom, and when we find people using their unique gifts and talents to do extraordinary things for others, we know that the Spirit is passing by.

Reflect on your last few days. Where did you see the Holy Spirit at work in those around you?

March 3

My beloved speaks and says to me:
"Arise, my love, my fair one,
and come away;
for now the winter is past,
the rain is over and gone.
The flowers appear on the earth;
the time of singing has come,
and the voice of the turtledove
is heard in our land.
The fig tree puts forth its figs,
and the vines are in blossom;
they give forth fragrance.
Arise, my love, my fair one,
and come away."
—Song of Solomon 2:10–13

The imagery of these verses always captivates me. I can sketch the scene in my mind: a terraced landscape touched with sunlight, white garden walls hung with flowering vines, the scent of jasmine, the throaty cooing of doves in the air. If I go further, I imagine myself meandering along the garden paths, invited by God, who walks with me. I'm not used to picturing myself as God's "beloved"—or vice versa—but something about the spring inspires me to try.

Read these verses again slowly. Fill your mind with the landscape of spring. Imagine that God is inviting you for a stroll.

March 4

Accept that some days you're the pigeon, and some days
you're the statue.
—Roger C. Anderson, *The Rotarian*

Many city parks feature a statue, standing tall with gravity
and authority, eyes fixed on some distant point. Yet one
often finds unmistakable evidence that the birds have paid
a visit, leaving white streaks that undermine the whole
effect.

Or do they? Even these dignified people had their
moments of weakness or struggle, moments when they
felt—pardon the expression—shat upon. We all do. The
pigeons remind us that even the people who enter the
history books are not immune to indignity or
embarrassment. It's a part of being human.

*Lord, help me to remember to live my life with grace
and humility.*

March 5

If I try to be like him, who will be like me?
—Yiddish proverb

It's easy to forget how unique we are as we grow up and see more of the world around us. We begin comparing ourselves to others and want what they have. It becomes tempting to think, "I have to be like her in order to be as fulfilled as she is."

But the body of Christ is made up of many parts, each of them essential and yet particular. The human family is a jigsaw puzzle. Each piece is both unique and uniquely vital; without one individual, the picture is not complete.

Lord, help me to see myself in the vastness of your creation as the unique and complex creature you made me to be. Help me to recognize my individuality and live it to the fullest.

March 6

Pray as you can, not as you can't.
—John Chapman

Sometimes, we fear that our prayers are not up to snuff, as if you need to do this prayer at this time of day with these words and in this posture. There's certainly value in trying various forms of prayer to find what resonates. But feeling the need to follow a certain practice can make prayer feel more like obligation than conversation.

As a teacher, I recognize that individual students learn best in different ways. Similarly, we individuals pray best in different ways. Whatever form of prayer speaks to you, relish it, and know that God loves to engage with you in the way that makes you most fully alive.

Spend a few moments thinking about what you do that makes you feel most in tune with God. Find a time to do it today, mindful of the presence of the creator.

March 7

The sky is the daily bread of the eyes.
—Ralph Waldo Emerson

Look up at the spring sky. Maybe you see blue, or gray, or white. Maybe you see coral and orange. No matter the details, you are looking at something that hasn't changed much over time.

Humans have altered the face of the planet, building towns and highways and dams. But the sky doesn't change. Yes, we send up airplanes and satellites; our vehicles add a film of smog that sometimes obscures our view. But really, we can't do anything to fundamentally change it. It's a potent reminder of our God: that no matter how much we mess up, there remains a goodness and beauty that no one can spoil.

The next time you step outside, take a moment to look long and hard at the unchanging immensity of the sky. Let your concerns settle into perspective.

March 8

We are God's work of art.
—Ephesians 2:10, *New Jerusalem Bible* translation

Some days I feel more like God's rough draft than a work of art. I am smudged, a not-yet-finished scribble. I'm not fit for display.

Maybe we're both the draft and the masterpiece at the same time. We all have edges that need to be touched up, impulses and negative feelings that need to be smoothed away.

God sees the best in us and can envision exactly how we'll look once that process is complete. The best part: we are cherished by God the whole way through. Even with our rough edges and smudges, God, making us, could never love us more.

God, thank you for loving me, even with all of my imperfections.

March 9

I have a hat. It is graceful and feminine and gives me a
certain dignity, as if I were attending a state funeral or
something. Someday I may get up enough courage to
wear it, instead of carrying it.
—Erma Bombeck

Breaking out of the routine can be daunting. Even minor
changes take effort. We find ourselves in a state of timid
stagnation, doing the "same old same old" when we owe it
to ourselves to shake it up a bit. But spring is not a time of
stagnation. Everything is changing around us.

It's time to paint our toenails blue, or try on that flashy
blouse, or experiment with a new kind of prayer, or bike
to work instead of driving. It makes us feel alive; there is
always something new to learn about ourselves.

*Think of one way you can shake up your routine. Resolve to
do it this week.*

March 10

Nothing is as obnoxious as other people's luck.
—F. Scott Fitzgerald

The German word *schadenfreude* means "a feeling of happiness at someone else's misfortune." It is often rooted in the assumption that there is only so much good fortune in the world. If others succeed, you won't. If they fail, your chances of success are greater.

Let's remember: God spreads an endless banquet and wants all of us to eat our fill. Someone else's heaping plate is not a sign that there is less for us; instead, it's proof of the abundant generosity of God, and there's enough of that to go around.

Think of an area in your life now where you are tempted toward schadenfreude. *See if you can pinpoint the reason why. Ask God to replace those feelings with trust that there is enough for all.*

March 11

When I was young, I admired clever people. Now that I
am old, I admire kind people.
—Abraham Joshua Heschel

I always seem to pick the slowest check-out line at the
supermarket. I stand with my groceries spread out on the
conveyer belt, waiting, while the person ahead of me tries
to pay with a sheaf of expired coupons or has a problem
with her credit card. My stress level climbs.

"I'm so sorry for the wait," the poor clerk finally says to
me. Here, I have a choice. I could give him an impatient
and clipped, "It's okay." Or I could breathe deeply, smile,
and say cheerfully, "It's fine. I'm not in any hurry." The
second option is much harder.

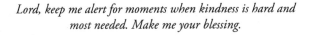

*Lord, keep me alert for moments when kindness is hard and
most needed. Make me your blessing.*

March 12

Look at the rainbow and praise him who made it;
it is exceedingly beautiful in its brightness.
It encircles the sky with its glorious arc;
the hands of the Most High have stretched it out.
—Sirach 43:11–12

A spring rainbow stops me in my tracks. I always feel as though I'm witnessing a miracle. One recent morning, as I pulled into the parking lot at school, I looked up to see a perfect rainbow spanning the campus. All around me, students were gazing up at the sky. In that moment, the routine sluggishness of morning was gone. Adults and teenagers alike were bowled over with wonder.

Technology has given us many shiny and brilliant things, but nature can always dazzle us more.

What's something you've seen that has made you feel a sense of wonder? Praise God for it.

March 13

Let them praise his name with dancing.
—Psalm 149:3

In spite of years of childhood ballet lessons, I'm a terrible dancer. I often joke that there are exactly two people in the world who think I'm a good dancer, and I gave birth to both of them. But when I see my sons giving in to the rhythms of the music on the radio, I can't *not* join them.

Whether it's the Jackson Five or Bill Haley and the Comets, my boys let the music carry them away, creating moves that are all their own. Their enthusiasm is infectious and it dissolves my self-consciousness. As I dance along with them, I'm grateful for the reminder that you don't have to do a thing well to do it joyfully.

What is something you love and yet avoid because of self-consciousness? Whether alone or with others, do it.

March 14

The palest ink is better than the best memory.
—Chinese proverb

I write down experiences I don't want to forget: my haircut on Thursday, things my kids have said and done, seeds of ideas for future articles or books. These are things I want to remember. I need pen and paper (or a keyboard) to keep them from fading into oblivion.

A written record is essential to keeping ideas alive. The evangelists knew this; in recording Christ's life, they altered human history. Our own records don't have that reach or resonance, but our scribbles are worth cherishing. They show us where we've been and where we still want to go.

Write down something that happened recently that you don't want to forget. Fold it up and tuck it away, knowing that someday, you'll find it again.

March 15

How very good and pleasant it is
when kindred live together in unity!
—Psalm 133:1

As the mother of young boys who are two years apart, I have refereed more than my share of squabbles. "He won't give me back my umbrella!" "He says this is his train, but it's really mine!" "He is spitting on me!" When I'm already stressed about the stacks of papers waiting to be graded or the fact that our refrigerator appears to be on strike, this kind of brotherly discord is particularly grating.

This psalm speaks to my mother's soul. It is indeed good and pleasant when the boys laugh together, when they collaborate joyfully on turning the bunk bed into a rocket ship. Savoring those moments of unity serves as a kind of defense against despair. When they squabble, I can be confident that they'll make their peace eventually, and I know from experience how sweet that peace will be.

Remember when your family last spent time together enjoying one another's company. Thank God for the experience.

March 16

You are a hiding place for me;
you preserve me from trouble;
you surround me with glad cries of deliverance.
—Psalm 32:7

"It's a monster! Hide!" my son yells gleefully, pointing at the bedroom door. My boys squeal and burrow under the blankets and pillows. They call to me to join them in safety, but it's the end of a long workday. I'm too exhausted to navigate the cavern of the covers.

All the same, I understand their desire for the safety of cover. There are plenty of times that I want to hide from my own anxieties, from my many obligations. Do I turn to God in those moments, or to something else: the Internet, chocolate, television? Though the Internet may seem like the easiest response, I can't deny that the outcome is best when I choose to burrow into the comfortable presence of God.

Lord, when the urge to hide from something overtakes me, remind me to turn to you. Surround me with your presence.

March 17

Sleep that knits up the ravell'd sleeve of care …
—William Shakespeare, *Macbeth*

There are many reasons why we women find a good night's sleep to be so elusive. The caffeine that gets us through our workdays can sabotage our nights. Money worries or health concerns often cause insomnia. There might be a newborn to a nrse or a six-year-old with an ear infection or a seventeen-year-old who is out on a date. With all these forces set to undermine a good night's rest, it's amazing we get any sleep at all.

As Shakespeare wrote, there's a spiritually renewing aspect to catching our z's. I find it easier to be positive, mindful, and charitable when I've had more than the bare minimum of rest. If there are small changes I can make to my routine that help me get more sleep, those are changes worth exploring.

Look objectively at your sleep habits this week. Resolve to make one small change to your routine in order to give yourself the gift of a refreshing night's sleep.

March 18

Television has proved that people will look at anything
rather than each other.
—Ann Landers

Technology dazzles and entertains; it also nudges me
toward sloth. It takes far more effort to play soccer with
my kids than it does to scroll through vintage tablecloths
on a website. But the rewards of real human interaction
are far greater than anything on a screen: the laughter of
my boys, their wiry bodies hurtling through space, the
sweet snapshot of a half hour on the lawn. These things
are tangible and real, and these spring afternoons won't be
around forever. I need to savor them while I can.

*When do you tend to mindlessly watch television or surf the
Internet? Set a reminder on your phone or your computer to
use that time instead to call a friend, to talk and to listen to
your spouse or kids, or to journal about a person who has
made a difference in your life.*

March 19

I am a camera with its shutter open, quite passive, recording, not thinking. Recording the man shaving at the window opposite and the woman in the kimono washing her hair. Some day, all this will have to be developed, carefully printed, fixed.
—Christopher Isherwood, *Goodbye to Berlin*

I have embraced a form of prayer called the Ignatian *examen*. It involves reviewing the day in God's presence, consciously identifying all the moments where I encountered God. God was in the driver who waved me ahead of her in traffic; in the sunlight touching the tops of the green hills; in the spontaneous hug from my younger son; in the cheerfulness of a coworker.

This form of prayer takes the random images I record during the day and develops them, helping me see their true contours and colors. I find that when I take the time to pray this way, an awareness of God's constant presence becomes beautifully fixed in my mind.

Review the last twenty-four hours. Where do you find God? Resolve to be more aware tomorrow as the day unfolds.

March 20

The music in my heart I bore,
Long after it was heard no more.
—William Wordsworth, "The Solitary Reaper"

Some tunes imprint themselves on our memories. At times this is a curse (how many obnoxious commercial jingles would we sooner forget?), but overall I count it as a blessing. Back in my running days, I'd mentally scroll through favorite Broadway show tunes as a way to keep my feet going even when I felt tempted to stop. While working in the kitchen, I occasionally find myself humming "Rhapsody in Blue" just for the joy of it, much as my younger son sings preschool tunes to himself when he is playing in his room.

At times like this, I recognize music as the gift that keeps on giving. A song that we hear and love sets down roots in our memory, guaranteeing that we can hear and love it again anytime we wish.

Identify a few of your favorite tunes, and say a prayer thanking God for the talents of those who fill the world with song.

March 21

How do you like to go up in a swing,
Up in the air so blue?
Oh, I do think it the pleasantest thing
Ever a child can do!
—Robert Louis Stevenson, "The Swing"

It was a mild evening, with shadows lengthening across the wide lawns of the park. I was sitting on a bench writing lesson plans when I noticed the empty swings. On a whim I chose one, sat down, stepped back a few paces, then let go. I pulled my legs out and in, gradually inching higher. In the still evening air I rediscovered the childhood joy of climbing into the sky, reaching the highest point and hanging there suspended for a thrilling half-second, then letting gravity pull me back down. There is no feeling on earth as carefree as that of soaring on a swing. Why don't I let myself feel this way more often?

A man walking along the path saw me and grinned. "Were there gaps in your childhood?" he asked jokingly.

No, I thought to myself, only in my adulthood.

Think of an activity that makes you feel truly joyful and carefree, and do it.

March 22

We cannot do everything, and there is a sense of
liberation in realizing that. This enables us to do
something, and to do it very well.
—Bishop Ken Untener

My husband jokingly refers to Mother Teresa Guilt: the
nagging sense we are failing if we don't move to a
developing country and devote our lives to helping the
poor. It is a common feeling among people who care
deeply about making the world a better place. But we aren't
all called to live like Mother Teresa. Those who are will
find their truest joy in serving as she did; those who aren't
will find their fulfillment elsewhere.

Perhaps your call is to help by teaching, organizing
a local book drive, caring for your children or an aging
parent, or using your artistic gifts to draw others closer to
the source of all creation. Discern how God is calling you
to serve others, and throw yourself into it joyfully.

*God, thank you for creating us to have so many different gifts
and abilities. Help me to use mine to make the world a more
peaceful place.*

March 23

Let everything that breathes praise the LORD!
Praise the LORD!
—Psalm 150:6

My husband runs the adult catechesis program at our parish. He was recently asked, "Why are there so many Bible verses about praising God? If God already knows he's 'the man,' why does he need us to keep telling him?"

I love Scott's answer: "When Ginny and I do something for our boys and then prompt them to say 'thank you,' it's not because we ourselves need to hear the words," he explained. "We say it because we want our boys to become people of thanks."

God knows that our lives are happier when we are constantly mindful that there is a creator who loves us and who made a world full of wonders for us to enjoy.

Make a list of things and people you love. Read the list aloud, stopping and praising God for each one.

March 24

No book is really worth reading at the age of ten which is not equally—and often far more—worth reading at the age of fifty and beyond.
—C. S. Lewis

Many books on prayer and spirituality have taken up residence on my shelves. But I'm finding that sometimes the greatest spiritual insights come from my kids' books. Often, they're the same books I read as a child. Yet, reading them again, now that I'm older and more experienced, is a true revelation.

Stone Soup celebrates the joy of community; *Ferdinand the Bull* is about choosing peace; *The Runaway Bunny* teaches the power of unconditional love; *Horton Hatches the Egg* is a parable about keeping one's word. There's a wealth of wisdom to be found on my kids' shelves, and I haven't outgrown my need for it.

Think of a book you loved as a child. Track down a copy at the library or bookstore. See what the story teaches you today.

March 25

Imagination grows by exercise, and contrary to common belief, is more powerful in the mature than in the young.
—W. Somerset Maugham

My sons love the picture book *Harold and the Purple Crayon* by Crockett Johnson. In the book, a little boy named Harold uses his magic purple crayon to draw anything he wants and needs. If he is hungry, he draws his favorite pies; if he needs to travel, he draws a boat.

On every page, Harold uses his crayon and his imagination to transcend the limits of reality, resulting in captivating adventures. He's a poster child for what is possible, and a kick in the pants for someone like me, who is often relentlessly practical and safe. Do I want the careful, predictable life—or do I want the nine kinds of pie and a boat? I don't have a magic purple crayon, true, but I do have an imagination. I must remember to use it.

Take time to write about a personal dream you have. Don't judge whether or not it is practical; just let yourself imagine it fully.

March 26

"For truly I tell you, if you have faith the size of a mustard seed, you will say to this mountain, 'Move from here to there,' and it will move; and nothing will be impossible for you."
—Matthew 17:20

It was my third pregnancy, and I was terrified. The first had been an ectopic, the second a miscarriage. As we waited for the ultrasound appointment that would reveal whether or not the child in my womb was alive, I wavered constantly between hope and despair. Two pregnancies, two losses; why should this one be any different?

But as we drove through the green Napa Valley, with yellow mustard plants bursting like sunlight out of the earth, I thought of Jesus' words. If he'd talked about faith the size of an oak or a redwood, I'd be out. But faith the size of a mustard seed? I could manage that.

Days later, we saw our baby. We nicknamed him Bud; months later, he became Matthew. He is my mustard-seed child, a reminder of what can grow from the very tiniest of beginnings.

Lord, I wish I had faith like a redwood, but so often I don't. Help me hold on to this mustard seed of trust and let it grow bigger in its own time.

March 27

To you do we send up our sighs, mourning and weeping
in this valley of tears.
—The Hail, Holy Queen prayer

I'm grateful my Catholic religion acknowledges the existence of brutal suffering. There have been moments of excruciating loss in my life that no mindfulness or cheerful efforts can overcome. News reports of tornadoes and massacres and war remind me that even though the world is a gorgeous place, it can also feel like a valley of tears.

In those moments, the image of Christ on the cross speaks to me as nothing else can. There are periods in every life when we feel as naked and vulnerable and racked with pain as Jesus on Calvary. We can't fast-forward through them; we can only endure them, trying to find some comfort in the love of others and in the knowledge that God has suffered, too.

Think of someone you know who is in pain. Offer a prayer, write a note of support, or do a concrete act of love to help him or her through this dark time.

March 28

Trouble is a part of your life, and if you don't share it, you
don't give the person who loves you a chance to love
you enough.
—Dinah Shore

During a part of my early teenage years, I struggled with
obsessive-compulsive disorder. Distressing thoughts would
get caught in my mind, rattling around like a coin in
a dryer. It was a silent battle, for the most part. I'd go
through long periods where the OCD didn't bother me,
only to have something randomly trigger the thoughts and
their attendant guilt.

When I started dating my husband, I was terrified
to share this with him. Finally, a few months into the
relationship, I did. His response was total love and
acceptance, which in turn gave me the courage to seek
counseling for the first time.

The sharing of my trouble wasn't the final chapter for
Scott and me, as I feared it might be; instead, it was the
start of a new kind of peace for me, and proof that I need
to give some people a chance to love me enough.

*God, thank you for the people who love us unconditionally
and help us move forward in our struggles.*

March 29

"Just the place to bury a crock of gold," said Sebastian. "I should like to bury something precious in every place where I've been happy and then, when I was old and ugly and miserable, I could come back and dig it up and remember."
—Evelyn Waugh, *Brideshead Revisited*

Sebastian has a much more cynical view of growing older than I do, but his idea speaks to me as much as it did when I chose this quotation for my college yearbook page. I love the idea of returning to places where I was happy, knowing that some little part of myself remains there.

It can be so easy to focus on the negative experiences of our past, to forget that the moments of pure joy play a vital role in making us who we are. I also like how Sebastian's words encourage mindfulness: we have to realize we are happy in order to bury the gold in the first place. There is an art to recognizing each happy moment for the treasure that it is.

Think back over the places you've been in your life. Which places would be the "crock of gold" stops on your personal pilgrimage?

March 30

I count myself in nothing else so happy
As in a soul rememb'ring my good friends.
—William Shakespeare, *Richard II*

Time spent with friends is one of the sacrifices on the altar of my busy life. I'm not proud of this, though I know why it happens. My family and my job demand so much of my energy that I can rarely summon the will to spearhead a girls' night out.

But when one of my friends does manage to get all of us in a restaurant booth at the same time, I always leave feeling a new kind of alive, a mid-spring blossom I'd forgotten about. These friendships feed a part of my soul that nothing else can, and it's only after these visits that I realize just how hungry I've been.

Look at your calendar. Mark off time to meet a friend for coffee or at least to call for a chat.

March 31

Know that even when you are in the kitchen, our Lord
moves amidst the pots and pans.
—St. Teresa of Ávila

Sometimes my kitchen is my little oasis, where I gaze out
over the rim of my coffee cup at the misty morning sky.
Other times, I'm frantically banging the lids onto bubbling
pots while snapping at anyone who enters my realm and
isn't helping. It is easy to feel God's presence during those
morning-sky moments, less so when my stress mounts to
a boil.

A brief prayer, even a prayer of just a few calming
breaths, can be very effective at turning down the heat. So,
too, can gratitude. I'm blessed to have this home, this food,
this family to feed. May I always remember that, especially
in the kitchen.

*Find a photograph or quotation that recalls God's presence for
you. Post it in a prominent place in the kitchen.*

April 1

The kiss of the sun for pardon,
The song of the birds for mirth,
One is nearer God's heart in a garden
Than anywhere else on earth.
—Dorothy Frances Gurney, "God's Garden"

I've spent time in many gardens. My mother's yard features beds of impatiens, marigolds, and primroses. My Grandma Wolf's garden has hollyhocks as tall as I am, and as children my sister and I would gleefully sip the honey from the honeysuckle climbing over her back fence. My Grandma Kubitz had no lawn, only paved terraces, but she always had planters full of azaleas, gardenias, bright begonias.

Different as they were, these gardens all shared something in common: each one had a small plaque featuring Gurney's verse tucked somewhere among the flowers. When I scroll back through my memories of these gardens, I remember the sweet honeysuckle and digging in the soil and sharing dinner on the patio with my grandparents on a warm spring night. This verse is just about right.

Think about a lovely garden or place of natural beauty that you have seen lately. Reflect on how you felt God's presence there.

April 2

Every rose is an autograph from the hand of the
Almighty God.
—Theodore Parker

The roses in California begin to bloom around the start
of April. In the winter those rose bushes were just bare
sticks. As the weeks passed, reddish leaves started to appear,
followed by tiny green buds, then glimpses of color. Until
one day I am dazzled by the glorious pink and orange and
white petals unfolding in perfect layers.

These rose bushes make me think of the ultimate
artist—God. They are God's masterpieces, yes; but they
are also God's autograph. They are a signature to cherish,
colorful proof that I have come face-to-face with the glory
of the creator.

*In your own life, what do you see as an autograph from the
hand of God—proof that God exists, and wants to engage
with you?*

April 3

I am always humbled by the infinite ingenuity of the Lord, who can make a red barn cast a blue shadow.
—E. B. White

When I took an art history class, we studied the techniques of great painters. We learned terms like *composition*, *scale*, and *perspective*; we studied the use of color in the works of Van Gogh and Picasso. The course gave me a new appreciation for the ways in which an artist creates an image that compels the gaze and evokes emotion in the viewer.

How often do I extend the same consideration to the artist God? There's splendid technique to be found in the perspective of the distant hills along the freeway, in the graded color of a sunset sky, in the contrasting textures of water and rock side by side in a stream. No artist can surpass the skill and passion of the creator.

The next time you step outside, pay attention to the artistry in the natural world around you.

April 4

There is no such thing in anyone's life as an
unimportant day.
—Alexander Woollcott

Life's milestones often involve special outfits: a wedding
dress, a graduation cap, a christening gown, a prom dress, a
new interview suit. You can usually tell a Big Day by what
a person is wearing.

Yet the days I spend in rumpled jeans and old pajamas
are every bit as important as the ones where I'm dolled up.
On these ordinary days all sorts of personal and familial
milestones take place: kids learn how to share, sibling
bonds are built, spouses discover new little things about
one another, parents learn to give without counting the
cost. These ordinary days may not make it into our photo
albums, but they make us who we are.

*Think of a recent day that strikes you as unimportant.
Consider what made it important after all.*

April 5

He who wants a rose must respect the thorn.
—Persian proverb

"What-If Land" is a pretty seductive place to visit. What if my job as an English teacher came without stacks of essays to grade? I'd love it if parenthood were all hugs and sweet bedtime stories and never involved a harrowing visit to the pediatric after-hours care. How great would it be if I could have my garden full of butterflies without having to spend time fighting the snails and weeds?

"What-If Land" is pure fantasy. Everything good comes with a cost; that's reality. I can find this depressing, or I can accept it and try not to complain, reminding myself that the rose is always worth the thorn.

Lord, help me to accept that there will be times when the gifts in my life don't feel like gifts.

April 6

Soon afterwards he went on through cities and villages, proclaiming and bringing the good news of the kingdom of God. The twelve were with him, as well as some women who had been cured of evil spirits and infirmities: Mary, called Magdalene, from whom seven demons had gone out, and Joanna, the wife of Herod's steward Chuza, and Susanna, and many others, who provided for them out of their resources.

—Luke 8:1–3

When we think of Jesus' companions, it's easy to focus on just the twelve men. Luke tells us that there were many women who accompanied Jesus as he traveled and preached. Much of the material help—the finances, food, and supplies needed to keep Jesus and his followers going—came not from men but from women. These verses show that even in the earliest days of Jesus' ministry, women played a crucial role in getting his message out to the world.

In a time when they were not encouraged to break out of narrow roles, many women recognized and responded to the transformative vision of Jesus, boldly giving their time, talent, and treasure to share that vision with others.

How do you use your time, talent, or treasure to spread the message of Jesus?

SPRING

April 7

If thou of fortune be bereft,
And in thy store there be but left
Two loaves—sell one, and with the dole
Buy hyacinths to feed thy soul.
—James Terry White, "Hyacinths"

Our decorating style at home can best be described as Early Modern Hand-Me-Down, with a motif of brightly colored plastic vehicles. But while the furniture doesn't match and there are toys constantly underfoot, our house usually features at least one vase of fresh flowers. In spring and summer, they come from my own garden; in the other seasons, I buy them at the grocery store.

I used to think this was a somewhat frivolous purchase, but I've gotten wiser since then. A vase of flowers can turn any room into a shrine honoring the beauty of creation. That's an investment worth making.

Treat yourself to a vase of flowers or some other sign of God's creative beauty.

April 8

When I stand before God at the end of my life, I would
hope that I would not have a single bit of talent left and
could say, "I used everything you gave me."
—Erma Bombeck

Years ago, I complimented my friend on the beautiful
red-rimmed china plates she had stacked on the sideboard.
"I use the good dishes and goblets a lot, even when I'm
eating alone," she said. "Otherwise, they'd sit in my
cupboard and I'd never see them."

I think of those dishes as a metaphor for talents. It's so
easy to keep our dreams and abilities hidden in the back
of a cabinet, where we don't have to expose them to public
view. But to die with untapped talents is like dying with
the china plates still in their original wrappers: it's wasting
a gift that was meant to be used and enjoyed.

*Lord, help me to recognize the less-obvious gifts you've given
me and put them to good use.*

April 9

In the morning, while it was still very dark, [Jesus] got up
and went out to a deserted place, and there he prayed.
—Mark 1:35

Having young kids, I am rarely alone with my thoughts.
Someone always needs a drink of water or a clean shirt or
urgent help getting the toy car out from under the sofa.
I've learned to be mindful of God's presence in all those
moments, even when I'm flat on my stomach sweeping
small vehicles and stale Cheerios out from underneath the
furniture.

But there are times when I turn to Scott and say, "I just
need a few minutes alone." I retreat to the bedroom and
close the door and lie down, staring at the light blue walls,
breathing in the silence. I could feel guilty for needing to
escape, but I don't. Even Jesus needed to get away from the
crowds every now and then, in order to re-ground himself
and come back to the world refreshed.

Identify a time when you can carve out some solitude today.
Take this time for yourself without guilt.

April 10

The virgin mother bore him in her womb, with love
beyond all telling . . .
—Preface to the Eucharistic Prayer,
Advent II, Roman Missal, 1973

Just about anything can be expressed with the right choice of words. Build a big enough vocabulary, I tell my students, and you can put words to any feeling. Yet I have to admit that some emotions and experiences defy description: they are too intense, too powerful for us to pin down with language.

I can't quite capture the glory of a just-opened rose, or the visceral love I have for my children. I do my best to write about them, but I always fall short. Instead of feeling frustrated, I've learned to recognize it as proof of the awesome, ineffable mystery that lies at the heart of all that is good.

Think of an experience that you could never put into words.
Thank God for the mysterious beauty of it.

April 11

"I got no God," he said.
"You got a God. Don't make no difference if you don't
know what he looks like."
—John Steinbeck, *The Grapes of Wrath*

As I enter my forties, this Steinbeck passage resonates with me more and more. There's so much I don't know about God. But I do believe that God exists, not just in my life but in everyone's life. My inability to grasp certain aspects of the divine doesn't mean that there is no God; instead, it invites me to remain open to the unexpected ways that God shows up in my life. If I knew exactly what God looked like, would I be so receptive to these surprises?

Probably not. Maybe that's the whole point.

For today, resolve to be open to the unexpected ways that God appears in your life.

April 12

To me every hour of the light and dark is a miracle,
Every cubic inch of space is a miracle.
—Walt Whitman, "Miracles"

I once thought miracles were flashy things that happened to people who lived long ago: the parting of the sea or Mary appearing to St. Bernadette in the grotto at Lourdes. Miracles were for others far away, not me.

Over the last few decades, I've realized that there are miracles everywhere. The birth of a child is a miracle; so too is the flowering of a bare branch in the spring, or the astonishing aerodynamics of a hummingbird, or the way that my son's elbow gradually heals itself after a run in with the blacktop at school. The miracles have always been there; what's new is my ability to see them.

Go through your day today or tomorrow looking for ordinary miracles.

April 13

"See, I am making all things new."
—Revelation 21:5

Is there a more perfect verse to express what happens in the spring? Everywhere we look, nature is showing off its newness: new buds, new lime-green leaves, new grass, new birds, new woodland mammals. It's a time to unwind the scarves and put away the gloves and enjoy having fewer layers between ourselves and the world.

We are free to get out and move more; the mild weather lets us take our exercise outside. And let's not forget spring cleaning, that satisfying ritual of removing the dust and clearing away the clutter. This is a season when everything around us nudges us to start something new.

Celebrate the spirit of spring by making a fresh start today.
Clean out a drawer, begin a new book, try a new recipe.

April 14

God is a comedian whose audience is afraid to laugh.
—H. L. Mencken

Many of us struggle to picture God having a sense of humor. Our default image of God is of a stern, unsmiling judge, someone who can kill with a glance and who never cracks a smile. And yet every one of us knows the power of a good laugh. We've all been rendered delightfully speechless by laughter, and we all know the relaxed, depleted-yet-happy feeling that comes afterward.

Why do we find it so hard to imagine God feeling the same? It's time to consider that maybe God gave us the ability to laugh because God knows firsthand just how marvelous it feels to do so.

The next time you laugh, imagine God laughing with you.

April 15

The baby has known the dragon intimately ever since he
had an imagination. What the fairy tale provides for him
is a St. George to kill the dragon.
—G. K. Chesterton, "The Red Angel"

Fairy tales were a feature of my childhood. I knew both the
sanitized Disney versions and the darker original stories,
some of which are very dark indeed. It is distressing to see
the villain prevail in the first part of the story, but there is
such satisfaction in the ultimate triumph of good over evil.

These days, life's antagonists aren't as obvious as a
jealous queen or a wicked stepmother. The dragons I fight
are more likely to be my own bad habits, my laziness, envy,
or pride.

I know that they can be defeated. After all, the fairy
tales have taught me that even the toughest dragon is no
match for a plucky, tenacious heroine who isn't afraid of a
little confrontation.

*Dear Lord, help me to recognize the dragons in my life and to
remember that you are stronger.*

April 16

In your light we see light.
—Psalm 36:9

The more I take time to register the presence of God and the more I thank God for the gifts in my life, the more gifts there seem to be. "Light" is the perfect way to describe it; when I'm mindful of the workings of God in my life, I am able to see everything more clearly.

Gratitude illuminates the world around me, showing me the blessings that are present even in the darkest, most obscure corners of my life.

Set your watch or timer to go off every hour. Then pause and be grateful for something in your life.

April 17

The act of writing is the act of discovering what
you believe.
—David Hare

It started in sixth grade, with a blank book that my aunt
sent me for my birthday. Since then, I've filled over thirty
volumes with my writing: big decisions, relationship
dramas, foreign travels, successes, failures. If I am ever
unsure how I feel about something, journaling always
offers clarity.

Even if we don't keep a physical journal, many of us
know the feeling of writing a long cathartic e-mail,
blogging about our experiences, or recording memories
in a baby book. The process delivers us to a different
emotional place than where we were when we began.
Writing isn't just a physical and mental activity; sometimes
it truly is a form of prayer.

*Recall an experience you need to process some more. Take ten
minutes to write about it.*

April 18

To eat is a necessity, but to eat intelligently is an art.
—François de La Rochefoucauld

I try to avoid a lot of fast food, but I have to admit that my diet consists largely of "fast eating." I rush to finish breakfast so I can get to work, where lunch is usually consumed swiftly at my desk between other tasks. Dinner tends to move at a slower speed, but I'm invariably distracted by a glass of spilled milk or leaping up to retrieve something I've forgotten in the kitchen.

How often do I eat mindfully—paying attention to what I'm putting into my mouth and relishing each different taste? Not often enough. Until I learn how to do that, I'll probably always be a certain kind of hungry.

The next time you eat something, pay attention to the experience and savor it.

April 19

And then my heart with pleasure fills,
And dances with the daffodils.
—William Wordsworth, "I Wandered Lonely as a Cloud"

My half-hour commute to work takes me past tall wooded hills and rolling grassy slopes, often dotted with grazing cows and horses. The trip is even lovelier in spring. Along one stretch of road, daffodils bloom for a few precious weeks—whole masses of them along both sides of the highway. It's a glorious pairing of color, the bright yellow against the vivid green grass, and I look forward to it every year.

English teacher nerd that I am, as I gaze at the flowers I always think of Wordsworth. You can't help but be happy when you are surrounded by such cheerful company, even on the daily commute.

Open my eyes, Lord, as I move through your creation. Help me to see and be filled with wonder. Every corner of your creation is filled with you.

April 20

Only love is creative.
—St. Maximilian Kolbe

These words offer guidance for what to do when we feel helpless, such as when someone close to us is suffering. What can we possibly say or do that will mitigate a friend's grief over a lost loved one, or will help a family member through a debilitating illness?

Our efforts, insignificant as they may seem, are in fact vitally important. A handwritten card, a homemade dinner, a bouquet of flowers, an offer to drive to the funeral home—all show the other person that he or she is loved. And though our actions feel like a tiny seed dropped into a vast field of suffering, those seeds have a creative and life-giving force.

Think of someone who has helped you lovingly during a difficult time. Offer a prayer of gratitude for him or her.

April 21

A mother keeps a vigil at the bedside of her sick child.
The world calls it "fatigue," but she calls it "love."
—Bishop Fulton J. Sheen

I never pulled an all-nighter in college. When I tried, I fell asleep around 2:00 a.m. The spirit was willing, but the flesh was weak. Parenthood, though, demands the occasional all-nighter. Every now and then your child suffers a raging earache, and an otherwise normal night becomes a miserable, timeless darkness for both of you. I'm not going to lie: those nights are one of the worst parts of being a parent.

These experiences remind me of how my own mother used to stay up with me when I was sick, caring for me without complaint. That helps me see the long march toward dawn for what it is: a chance to imitate the woman I admire the most.

Think of some kind act your mother did for you. Do it cheerfully for someone else.

April 22

Some give freely, yet grow all the richer;
others withhold what is due, and only suffer want.
A generous person will be enriched,
and one who gives water will get water.
—Proverbs 11:24–25

So many Bible passages about generosity turn common sense right on its ear. If you give away what you have, doesn't that mean you have less? If you save things for yourself, doesn't that mean you end up with more? Not necessarily.

Scripture challenges us to see that the opposite is often true: generosity creates generosity, and those who give actually receive. It challenges us to share what we have with others, whether it's our time or our financial resources or our energy or our talents. When we do, we discover that when we think we're subtracting, we're really multiplying.

My God, you give so freely! Let me always remember your generosity and use it as a model for my own.

April 23

Yet I should kill thee with much cherishing.
—William Shakespeare, *Romeo and Juliet*

Whether it's a child or a spouse or a friend, often our instinctive way of showing affection is to shower him or her with constant attention. Yet there are times when the best way to show love is to back off for a while. If my husband doesn't readily respond to my questions about his day, maybe it's my cue to retreat and give him a little bit of alone time. When my boys become teenagers who crave independence, I'll have to restrain my natural instinct to give them a huge public hug as I drop them off at school.

What we see as care can sometimes be received as smothering, and a relationship is always healthiest when each person in it has space to grow.

Lord, help us to be sensitive to the needs of others and to recognize their boundaries, even when it's hard.

April 24

Every pair of eyes facing you has probably experienced
something you could not endure.
—Lucille Clifton

I have this monologue more often than I care to admit:

> That woman has such a charmed life. She's always well dressed
> and her hair is perfect. Her kids are neat and well behaved,
> they have a gorgeous house, and their car is always clean. It
> must be great to have it so easy.

I constantly remind myself of Lucille Clifton's words. How
much do I really know about this woman's life? There are
struggles in her past—maybe even in her present—that I
can't see. If I knew what they were, I would more likely
admire her not for her perfect hair and house, but for her
courage and resilience. May I always remember that.

*The next time you envy someone's charmed life, remind
yourself that everyone has struggles and is in need of
compassion.*

April 25

The wearer best knows where the shoe pinches.
—Irish proverb

More than once, I've received advice from people who think they know my life better than I do. It's always annoying, but before I get too critical, I have to admit that I sometimes do the same. It's easy to impose my own wisdom onto someone else's life, eagerly assuming that what worked for me will work for her. A friend isn't happy with her prayer life? A new mom can't get her baby to sleep through the night? An earnest desire to help can sometimes morph into a one-size-fits-all prescription that offers little real assistance.

Sharing our experiences is a key part of friendship, but so too is the compassionate recognition that every person's life is different.

Lord, today help me to listen more than I advise.

April 26

Where you tend a rose, my lad,
a thistle cannot grow.
—Frances Hodgson Burnett, *The Secret Garden*

When our spiritual lives feel dull and our creative lives seem flat, it's worth thinking about what we are feeding our souls. Are we reading books that expand our understanding of humanity, or does our literary diet leave us feeling empty? Do our free evenings include some time for quiet dreaming, or are they hijacked by the relentless noise of television?

I'm not saying that some of these pastimes are good and some aren't. I'm only saying that it's worth reflecting upon which activities inspire us to think and wonder and create. When we dedicate our leisure time to those pursuits, it can help us draw closer to the greatest creator of all.

Take some time—even if it's only a few minutes—to do something today that celebrates beauty and creativity.

April 27

*I like trees because they seem more resigned to the way
they have to live than other things do.*
— Willa Cather, *O Pioneers!*

Trees are especially beautiful in spring, with their
eye-catching clean green foliage, new shoots and flowers.
Tall trees provide shelter and perspective, reminding us
that we're not the biggest creatures out there. A tree has age
and resilience, having survived storms, high winds, and the
passage of time.

The rooted solidity of a tree offers wisdom for our own
lives. We can take steps to create our own destinies, but
there are circumstances in every life that we can't change,
circumstances that we can only accept. There is something
noble about learning how to flourish in place the way the
trees do.

*Think of a situation in your life that you can't change. Pray
for the grace to accept it and to even flourish in that place.*

April 28

The believer in God has to account for the existence of
unjust suffering; the atheist has to account for
everything else.
—Milton Steinberg

If you believe in God, sooner or later you bump up against
the question of why bad things happen. To be honest,
every explanation I've ever heard feels a little bit off. I don't
know why suffering happens; I wish I did. But somehow,
it seems like a bigger challenge to have to explain all the
good things: how the world got here in the first place;
how an entirely new person can come into being simply
through the physical love of two people; how the sun rises
each day without fail; how a redwood can live for two
thousand years.

In the final analysis, I'm with Milton Steinberg. Belief
in God provides me with many more answers than
questions.

What in your life helps you believe in the existence of God?
Make a list.

April 29

Sometimes our light goes out but is blown again into
flame by an encounter with another human being. Each
of us owes deepest thanks to those who have rekindled
this inner light.
—Albert Schweitzer

In times of doubt or difficulty, sometimes we retreat from
others. We give ourselves different reasons. *It's too
depressing to be with me right now,* we think. Or, *I'm
ashamed at having these problems.* Or, *No one can help me,
so I won't even ask.*

We forget that when the situation is reversed and
someone we love is struggling, we want nothing more than
to help. It can be uncomfortable to let other people into
our troubles, but sometimes we need to. We need to admit
that our light is out, and let them offer their breath to
bring it back to life.

*Think of a time when your light was out. Thank God for the
person who helped rekindle it.*

April 30

Work is love made visible.
—Kahlil Gibran, *The Prophet*

Most evenings find me standing at the kitchen counter packing lunch boxes for the next day. It's been a major feature of my routine for the past three years, and I sometimes think that if my life had a theme song, that song would be called "Cutting the Crusts Off Sandwiches." It's highly boring and, frankly, navigating the different tastes of two boys is a real pain.

Can I challenge myself to think of this as an expression of my deepest maternal feelings? Can I see this lunch as love made visible, snapped into a plastic container and zipped into a robot-themed lunch box? In the words of one of my boys' beloved storybook characters, "I think I can."

Choose a least favorite chore. Reframe it in your mind as love made visible.

May 1

Doubt isn't the opposite of faith; it is an element of faith.
—Paul Tillich

If we're honest, nearly all of us has had a period where it's not so easy to believe. At times faith feels like an easy garden stroll. At other times faith feels like walking headlong into a stiff wind, when all we can do is hang on to our hats and keep on slogging.

I like when people write about the serene garden moments, but I like it even more when they write about doubt. It normalizes my own feelings and allows me to be completely honest with myself. Even better, their hard-won wisdom becomes a windbreaker that I can tuck away and pull out whenever I need it, making my own slog a little bit easier.

Next time you feel doubts in your faith life, don't be afraid to share them with others.

May 2

In those days Mary set out and went with haste to a
Judean town in the hill country, where she entered the
house of Zechariah and greeted Elizabeth. When
Elizabeth heard Mary's greeting, the child leaped in
her womb.
—Luke 1:39–41

When I had two small children, I realized the size of the
United States. The cross-country flight to visit my in-laws
meant navigating a double stroller through the security
checkpoint, figuring out how much formula would be
allowed on board, and removing a foul diaper on a plane
with no pull-down changing table.

Mary didn't have quite the same issues when she visited
her cousin, but she still had to get her pregnant self across
hilly, rocky terrain—without restrooms and snack bars.
The fact that she went "in haste," not letting the
discomforts of the journey stop her, is an inspiration to
me. It's a reminder that even the most challenging journey
doesn't last forever, and that family always waits joyfully on
the other side.

*Lord, when I get bogged down in the difficulties of my own
journey, let me be mindful of Mary's resolve.*

May 3

> And as [Jesus] sat at dinner in the house, many
> tax-collectors and sinners came and were sitting with
> him and his disciples. When the Pharisees saw this, they
> said to his disciples, "Why does your teacher eat with
> tax-collectors and sinners?"
> —Matthew 9:10–11

It's easy to create barriers between ourselves and others. We unconsciously use a difference in religion, political party, style of dress, or even a favorite baseball team as a reason to assume that we have nothing in common with a new acquaintance.

That's why Jesus is such a powerful witness. Even the strongest social barriers of his time crumbled in the face of his desire to forge a real connection with those around him. And if we follow his example, we too may find new friendships being born in surprising places.

Think of someone you have unconsciously dismissed as being
"not friend material." Next time you encounter him or her,
look for the common ground you share.

May 4

You have kept count of my tossings;
put my tears in your bottle.
Are they not in your record?
—Psalm 56:8

I am struck by the vividness of the imagery in this verse.
Think of it! God has saved every one of our tears,
remembers every growing pain from our past.

Parents save artifacts as their children grow up: the little
wristband from the hospital, a lock of hair from the first
haircut, the preschool drawings of people with small round
faces and long spidery limbs, the photocopied program
from a dance recital. Our kids grow up so fast, and these
mementos are a way of keeping their earliest years vividly
alive to us.

I imagine God saves our tears not because it is pleasant
to look back on our suffering, but because God keeps
track of every milestone on our way into maturity. We
may forget who we used to be, but God the loving parent
never does.

*Take some time to revisit a memento of your past. Meditate
on your own growth since that time.*

May 5

Then she strolled into the park. The park was always a pleasure. She was in a thoughtful mood, and the soft green shadowed silence lured her. . . . And she was in a listening and dreaming mood—one of the moods in which bird, leaf, and wind, sun, shade, and scent of growing things have part.
—Frances Hodgson Burnett, *The Shuttle*

A walk alone has a particularly meditative flavor in the evening. As the day draws to a close, we meander slowly, letting the impressions of the day sink into our bones. We can process the big events, as if the movement of our feet awakens understanding.

These evening strolls are especially renewing in springtime as we see new growth in the branches and flower beds all around us. If the day has failed to live up to its promise, a spring evening offers assurance that good things are just waiting to bloom.

Take an evening stroll, even if it's only for a few minutes, and see where your thoughts lead you.

May 6

Flowers are the sweetest things that God ever made, and
forgot to put a soul into.
—Henry Ward Beecher, *Life Thoughts*

When I've had a chance to plant the first annuals of the
year, my yard feels instantly more dynamic, as if guests
have finally arrived for a party. I feed them with fertilizer
and offer them water and look after their general
happiness, and in return, they fill the yard with color
and life.

They don't have souls, but they certainly do wonders
for mine.

Plant flowers in the yard or buy a bouquet for your table.
Savor the way that they make your house feel more alive.

May 7

"Why must people kneel down to pray? If I really wanted to pray I'll tell you what I'd do. I'd go out into a great big field all alone or in the deep, deep woods, and I'd look up into the sky—up—up—up—into that lovely blue sky that looks as if there was no end to its blueness. And then I'd just feel a prayer."
—L. M. Montgomery, *Anne of Green Gables*

As a child, I had two little china figurines that someone gave me as a gift. One was a little girl and one was a little boy, and both were kneeling in prayer, hands together and eyes closed. That posture is the one we most associate with prayer, but it's hardly the only one.

Sometimes standing out in nature with our eyes wide open, Anne-style, is the best way to communicate with God. Many of us feel most open to God when we lie down to pray, or we find that God seems closest when we sketch or dance. We can do things with our bodies that make our souls feel more alive. These actions are worth exploring.

Try praying in a new posture today. How does it feel?

May 8

It is better to deserve honors and not have them than to
have them and not deserve them.
—Mark Twain

It's always gratifying when a local radio or television station
takes a few minutes to highlight someone in the
community who has lived a life of service for others:
tutoring at-risk children or serving the homeless or
sheltering stray pets. The stories are usually shoehorned in
at the end of the program, with the prime airtime going
to politicians and famous athletes, but they're nonetheless
a reminder of the thousands of people who, without
recognition or applause, quietly do things that matter.

In our own lives, each of us could rattle off the names
of ordinary people who have supported, loved, challenged,
cared for, sacrificed for, and inspired us. They don't expect
awards or publicity for what they do, but we can still honor
them by saying thanks.

*Who deserves an award for his or her role in your life? Write
that person a note of thanks.*

May 9

If you fear the Father, go to the Son. If you fear the Son,
go to the Mother.
—St. Bernard of Clairvaux

When I interviewed women for my book *Mary and Me*, I discovered a common theme: the approachability of the mother of Jesus. Several women talked about times when, due to past mistakes or bad childhood theology, they felt too intimidated to speak to God or to Jesus. Mary was different; she felt more accessible, like a calm and nonjudgmental mother.

And as they developed a relationship with Mary, they found that it didn't end there. In often surprising ways, Mary became the bridge that led them over their fear and into a closer relationship with her Son.

*Reflect on Mary: such a proud mother. What would she like
you to know about her Son?*

May 10

> The world is so full of a number of things,
> I'm sure we should all be as happy as kings.
> —Robert Louis Stevenson, "Happy Thought"

Once, I sat at a café table writing out a list of things I love. The list filled pages of my notebook, and making it was a remarkably addictive exercise.

My list was diverse: libraries, blue hydrangeas, British comedy, Irish accents. It was fascinating to see how one thing led to another. It was a tangible and welcome reminder of how many things in my life really do bring me joy.

Sit down and number a paper from one to fifty. Make a list of things you love.

May 11

Mankind will not die for lack of information; it may perish
for lack of appreciation.
—Abraham Joshua Heschel, *Who Is Man?*

I was walking briskly around a local park one morning,
when something compelled me to try a new path. It was
lined on both sides with Japanese maple trees. They were
among the tallest I'd ever seen, with firm solid trunks, and
their branches met and touched a few feet above my head.
It was like walking through a tunnel of green lacework,
with bits of light breaking through the leaves. Simply being
in that sanctuary was a balm to my spirits.

How many times had I been to this park over the years
and never even seen these trees?

I don't dwell on my past blindness. I'm appreciating
them now, and that is what matters.

*In a place that you feel you know by heart, look for something
new to appreciate.*

May 12

"Would you not be happier if you tried to forget her severity, together with the passionate emotions it excited? Life appears to me too short to be spent in nursing animosity, or registering wrongs."
—Charlotte Brontë, *Jane Eyre*

Forgiving others is hard work. It can feel like a tacit approval of a person's bad behavior; it seems to run counter to our desire for justice to be done. Sometimes, too, a grudge against another person becomes so much a part of our identity that it would be frightening to remove it.

Yet those who study forgiveness and its emotional effects report that it is a critical step in achieving personal happiness. Instead of keeping us cramped in place, forgiveness stretches us in healthy ways. It's not easy and it may not feel natural, but it is a spiritual workout that ends up making us feel fully alive.

Identify someone in your life whom you would like to forgive. Pray for the will to do it.

May 13

"There is nothing like staying at home for real comfort."
—Jane Austen, *Emma*

Is your home a sanctuary, a place where you enjoy spending time? Or is it a sterile outpost where you return periodically to eat, sleep, and bathe before heading out to do your "real living" elsewhere?

Not everyone is a homebody, but there is something to be said for making your living space a place where you like to be. This spring, take a look at your home. Is it cluttered and chaotic? Is that old paint just too depressing? Have you never really unpacked the boxes from your last apartment?

You don't have to call in a designer to the stars or spend a lot of money to make minor changes. Give several of your unused belongings to charity, clean a few windows, take some time to display favorite photos on your dresser. Make your physical space a little more comfortable, and feel your spirit respond.

Do one small thing today that makes you feel happier about being at home.

May 14

Happiness is the settling of the soul into its most
appropriate spot.
—Aristotle

The sweet spot in tennis is the area right in the middle of
the racket and down a bit. When the ball makes contact
in the sweet spot, there's a satisfying *zwing!* sound, and the
ball goes sailing over the net at high speed.

Though I don't play tennis anymore, other things in life
occasionally give me that glorious sweet-spot feeling. I get
it when I write something that says exactly what I mean,
or when I have a great day in the classroom, or when I am
fully present in sharing a fun experience with my boys.

These sweet-spot moments don't come every day, but
they always give me energy that lasts.

*Think of a past "sweet-spot" moment in your life. How did it
feed your soul? How can you recapture or re-create the sense of
exhilaration?*

SPRING

May 15

To be hopeful in bad times is not just foolishly romantic.
It is based on the fact that human history is a history not
only of cruelty, but also of compassion, sacrifice,
courage, kindness.
—Howard Zinn, *You Can't Be Neutral on a Moving Train*

I've heard people make comments such as "Humans are innately cruel." Or, "Why do you think there have been so many wars? Because it's part of our nature to want to dominate others." But there is an antidote to this pessimism, and it lies in remembering the people who have dedicated their lives to affirming the rights and dignity of others. A few names that come to mind are Mother Teresa, Cesar Chavez, Harriet Tubman, Oskar Schindler, Oscar Romero, Dorothy Day, and Martin Luther King Jr.

We don't have to consult the history books to find heroes closer to home, too. Each of us has encountered people who, even in hard times, freely show compassion and kindness. Whether they are famous or not, these people are compelling evidence that we shouldn't accept bad behavior as normal.

Take the time today to read about a person whose courage
and compassion you admire.

May 16

There are more things in heaven and earth, Horatio,
Than are dreamt of in your philosophy.
—William Shakespeare, *Hamlet*

While my dear friend Mary was dying of cancer, we frequently talked about heaven. "What is heaven like?" she wondered aloud in the last few months of her life, sometimes with a great sense of urgency.

Ultimately, I think our limited human experience bumps up against the vast mysteriousness that is God, and we realize that our understanding simply can't go any further. That's why I think the best answer came from our pastor, Father Xavier: "Mary, I honestly don't know what heaven is going to be like," he told her a few weeks before her death. "But I do know this: it has to be way better than we could ever imagine."

Think about what you don't know. Let yourself rest in the mystery.

May 17

You are constantly invited to be what you are.
—Ralph Waldo Emerson

The word *invitation* is lovely. It tells us that the person on the receiving end has a choice about whether to respond. It also hints that there's something desirable about what is being offered.

This quotation reminds us that every day is an invitation to start living as our truest, most authentic selves. Will we recognize this invitation for the great opportunity that it is? And will we recognize that God, who wants our deepest joy, is the One who issues it?

What would it mean to live your own life more authentically?

May 18

I have called you by name, you are mine.
—Isaiah 43:1

One of the most important things a teacher can do at the start of the school year is to learn her students' names quickly. Calling someone by name is a form of recognition and validation, and often is the first step in building a relationship.

Even when you know someone well, there is power in using a person's name. When a friend, family member, or colleague starts a comment with *Ginny*, I tend to pay more attention. The mere mention of my name reminds me of our relationship and makes the request feel more personal.

So many of our interactions today are distant and can feel impersonal. Calling someone by name is a subtle but meaningful way to express a connection.

For the rest of the day, make a point to call people by their names. See how it feels. Watch their reactions.

May 19

Mary Magdalene went and announced to the disciples,
"I have seen the Lord."
—John 20:18

There's such an adrenaline rush that comes from sharing good news with others. Mary thought Jesus was dead forever, and suddenly he is there in the flesh. Could there be a greater joy?

Jesus tells her to go and tell the apostles that he is alive. I can imagine Mary taking off at a run, practically flying in her excitement, overwhelmed with eagerness to spread her astonishing news. This is why she's often called the "apostle to the apostles." She brought the good news to those who would later spread it around the globe, and she showed them how it's done.

What good news can you share with a friend today?

May 20

The year's at the spring
And day's at the morn;
Morning's at seven;
The hill-side's dew-pearl'd;
The lark's on the wing;
The snail's on the thorn;
God's in his heaven—All's right with the world!
—Robert Browning, "Pippa's Song"

At times my mornings involve digging frantically through laundry baskets to find a clean pair of pants for my son, while looking at my watch and realizing I should have left for work five minutes earlier. Or I drive one block from home and have to turn around because I forgot the coffee, without which I cannot make it through the day. Mornings often make me feel frantic, scattered, snappish with my family—anything but serene.

Maybe "God's in his heaven, all's right with the world" could become my new mantra. Or perhaps I could tweak it and make it more comforting still: "God's in this household, all's right with the world!"

Lord, you are here, all's right with the world. Help me to remember that when I'm most frazzled.

May 21

"Why do we call all our generous ideas illusions, and the mean ones truths?"
—Edith Wharton, *The House of Mirth*

One evening, when the boys and I were talking about our upcoming camping trip, my son had a novel idea about what to do with my husband's extra tent. "You know what I'm going to do?" he said across the dinner table. "I'm going to drive all around the country, and when I find someone who doesn't have a house, I'm going to give them Daddy's other tent."

"What a nice thing to do," I said to him. Inside, of course, I thought, *Oh, kids—they have the sweetest and the most impractical ideas.*

But maybe my son is the wise one. Maybe I've lost something in my adult pragmatism: a sense of what is possible and of what is truly worth doing.

Next time you are with a child, listen seriously to what he or she has to say. Appreciate the insight there.

May 22

Grief is the price we pay for love.
—Queen Elizabeth II

The loss of a loved one can make even the abundance of spring feel lifeless. In the middle of devastating grief, not much seems to help. All we can do is let ourselves feel what we feel and take solace in the presence of friends who are willing to walk through the pain with us. We can also take comfort in the words that Queen Elizabeth shared at a memorial service for 9/11 victims: Grief is the price we pay for love.

Our mourning shows that we opened our souls to another person; that we accepted the future cost because we knew that it was well worth paying. Life offers a choice between love and loss or nothing, and our grief is proof that we made the right choice.

Pray today for a person you know who is grieving the loss of someone they loved.

May 23

Listening is a magnetic and strange thing, a creative
force. The friends who listen to us are the ones we move
toward, and we want to sit in their radius. When we are
listened to, it creates us, makes us unfold and expand.
—Karl Menninger

Think of a good listener you know. How do his or her
facial expressions and posture and words show
attentiveness? How does his or her quiet focus make
you feel?

The experience of being listened to—truly listened
to—is rare. And yet there's a reason why good listeners
seem to be so well liked. At our core, each of us wants
to be heard and recognized and understood. When we
aren't afraid of being interrupted or of boring our listener,
we may articulate things that we didn't understand before.
That's why, ultimately, good listening is a gift to the person
speaking. It's also an invitation for the speaker to respond
in kind.

*The next time you have a conversation with someone, focus
on truly listening to her words instead of trying to plan your
response in advance.*

May 24

The ordinary arts we practice every day at home are of
more importance to the soul than their simplicity
might suggest.
—Thomas Moore

My grandmother, who is in her nineties, has spent the
vast majority of her life as a homemaker. Her résumé
showcases an impressive array of domestic arts. She has
perfected the making of peach pie and Christmas stollen.
She maintains a mostly gopher-free vegetable garden. She
makes dolls and teddy bears and crocheted afghans. She
constantly updates her photo albums, providing endless
entertainment to family members who love to see
themselves in the pages.

She enjoys these activities thoroughly, and she's one of
the most contented people I know. When I think of her,
I reflect upon the two parts of the word "homemaker." I
think about how beautiful it is to know how to make a
house a home.

*Think of something you do at home, such as cooking,
mending, gardening, or organizing. Start thinking of it as an
art rather than a task.*

May 25

Set me as a seal upon your heart,
as a seal upon your arm;
for love is strong as death,
passion fierce as the grave.
—Song of Solomon 8:6

A mother wears a bracelet with a dangling silver charm for each of her children. A wife wears a wedding ring. A college student wears a cross given to her by her parents at her confirmation and earrings that once belonged to her favorite aunt.

Like the seal mentioned in the Bible verse, these pieces of jewelry are tangible symbols of relationships. It comforts us to wear them against our skin and see them flash before our eyes as we bend to unload groceries or grab a subway strap. These seals remind us that no matter where we go, the love of others always goes with us.

Put on a piece of jewelry or an accessory that reminds you of another person. Make a point of thinking of that person throughout the day.

May 26

For Mercy has a human heart,
Pity a human face,
And Love, the human form divine,
And Peace, the human dress.
—William Blake, "The Divine Image"

Take a few moments to think of the virtues that people in your life possess. When you think of generosity, who comes to mind? When you imagine listening without judgment, who in your family comes closest to embodying that? Is there anyone in your community of friends or colleagues who personifies wisdom?

This exercise reminds us that these virtues are not just abstract ideas. We get to know virtues not by studying books, but by seeing them lived out well in the messy, real world around us.

Identify a virtue that your friends and family would associate with you. Spend some time today trying to live it out more intentionally.

May 27

What one has to do usually can be done.
—Eleanor Roosevelt

"I have absolutely no idea how I'm going to get this all done," I tell my husband. A writing deadline, final exams to grade, the boys' doctor's appointments and swimming lessons, the fact that Scott will be away all weekend—just thinking of it all, my breathing becomes more shallow and my pulse rate increases. It's fight-or-flight response. I'm not running from a tiger in the jungle, but I do feel threatened by all that I have to do and dubious about making it out alive.

At these moments I have to stop, breathe, and take the long view. I've felt this way before, and I've lived to tell about it. I can't do everything I want to do—cleaning the bathroom and visiting the library will wait—but I can surely do what is absolutely necessary. For now, that's accomplishment enough.

The next time you feel overwhelmed, think of the stress you've survived in the past. Let that give you confidence.

May 28

Friends who count . . . don't.
—Robert Plunkett

When it comes to my family's division of labor, I have a tendency to keep mental score. I bathed the kids three nights in a row; it's Scott's turn now. I cooked dinner; why doesn't he offer to clean the bathroom?

I find the same tendency creeping into my relationships with friends. Why am I always the one to suggest getting together? I overlook the plank in my own eye when it comes to reaching out to friends; I'm not nearly as good in that area as I'd like to think.

Sure, no relationship can be totally one-sided. It's not healthy when one person makes all the effort. But a mental tally of grievances hinders more than it helps. Generosity of spirit, or an honest conversation about how best to reconnect, can get the focus off the scoreboard and back onto the relationship, where it belongs.

Lord, help me be aware of my tendency to keep score. Help me to remember that there is no score, only abundance and generosity.

May 29

A book is like a garden carried in the pocket.
—Chinese proverb

I don't mind a long wait—at the DMV, at the doctor's office, or anywhere else—as long as I have a book in my purse. No matter where I happen to be, opening a book is like entering a portable world, a place where the story leads down winding roads and ideas begin to take root in the subconscious. In this world, I encounter characters who astonish with their boldness or quirkiness. I also find characters in whom I recognize myself, for good or for bad.

A book is much more than just ink on paper; it's something with a life of its own, and it invites us to ponder our own lives more deeply.

Make a list of five books that have touched your life. Resolve to reread one of them in the near future.

May 30

The grey-eyed morn smiles on the frowning night,
Chequering the eastern clouds with streaks of light.
—William Shakespeare, *Romeo and Juliet*

There is something magical about witnessing the shift from darkness to light, when for a brief moment day and night coexist. Then the night is gone and sunlight drenches the landscape.

When we feel apprehensive about shifts and changes in our routine, it's worth remembering that every day of our lives begins with a transition from one extreme to another: a surprisingly gentle one, but a dramatic transition nonetheless.

Is there a change to your routine you are anxiously anticipating? Did something happen today that you didn't plan? Rest easy, recognizing it as the way of the world.

May 31

We do not remember days, we remember moments.
—Cesare Pavese

It's a common writing and prayer exercise to imagine your perfect day. In reality, we know that there's no such thing. Each day is a mix of both the frustrating and the renewing, the dull and the exhilarating, the painful and the pleasant.

There's something comforting about this fact. It means that a day that is going poorly has the potential to be redeemed by one gloriously perfect moment. That moment can sustain us for quite a while.

Make a list of the beautiful moments you've had this spring.

Summer

Jessica Mesman Griffith

I'm decidedly not the summer type. I don't tan, I burn. I wilt in the heat.

But this year, I need summer badly. Our family was homeless for a time, thanks to a freak storm that destroyed the second story of our house. Each month brought some new challenge or crisis for my husband, my children, or me. I need time to rest and repair. I want to meditate on goodness and abundance.

The themes of summer—maturity and fruition, leisure and play, reunion and separation—speak to my own current season of life as a woman and to my most pressing spiritual questions. I'm approaching midlife, but this is the first year I've thought, *I am grown. What now?*

These meditations attempt to answer that question. I drew inspiration from the summer feasts and saints of the church, Scripture, poetry, and my children's favorite stories.

June 1

Be praised, my Lord, through all Your creatures,
especially through my lord Brother Sun,
who brings the day; and You give light through him.
And he is beautiful and radiant in all his splendor!
Of You, Most High, he bears the likeness.
—St. Francis of Assisi

Vincent van Gogh moved to Arles in the south of France
due to his poor health and experienced a dramatic
improvement. He felt spiritually invigorated, as if the
world were "enchanted." This proved the beginning of the
most fertile period of his short career.

Many of his paintings at Arles—*Sunflowers*, *The
Sower*—are charged with the golds and oranges of the
region's deep summer sun, glowing like molten iron. The
sun inspires growth and healing, wakes the sleeping, and
coaxes the dormant seed from the earth. He wrote to his
brother Theo that those who don't believe in the sun are
infidels. Why? Because for him, as for St. Francis, the sun's
light reflects the light of God.

*Let the sun warm, restore, and inspire you today. See the sun
and the sunflowers as Van Gogh did, as proof of God's
ongoing action in our world.*

June 2

Growth [is] the only evidence of life.
—John Henry Cardinal Newmann, quoting Thomas Scott

Summer is a wonderful time to see the truth of this statement. We see growth all around us in the verdant trees and the overgrown vegetable gardens. As nature thrives and grows, we see evidence of God's life all around us.

But God is also alive within us, and we too must grow and change. God grows and lives in us when we push out further and further into the unknown, beyond our comfortable, carefully manicured plot; when we take risks and leaps of faith; when we long to see who God wants us to become.

How is God growing in me today? What can I do to grow God's presence in the world?

June 3

Consider the lilies, how they grow: they neither toil nor spin; yet I tell you, even Solomon in all his glory was not clothed like one of these. But if God so clothes the grass of the field, which is alive today and tomorrow is thrown into the oven, how much more will he clothe you—you of little faith!
—Luke 12:27–28

How do wildflowers grow? No gardener tends or fertilizes or propagates them. And yet they bloom and thrive in drainage ditches and piles of gravel on our country road. Wildflowers are the opposite of worry and toil. They are a picture of trust.

We know what Jesus thinks of wildflowers. He says their raiment is more beautiful than the richest king's. If God cares for the plants growing wild near my road, then he cares infinitely more for us. We are God's most treasured creation, designed for eternity. He is committed to our care.

Lord, it is almost impossible for me to stop worrying about what the future holds. But you know my needs better than I do. Fill me with confidence that you will provide.

June 4

These wonders are brought to our own door.
—Ralph Waldo Emerson, *Nature*

I opened the door one afternoon to find my neighbor holding a tiny, mewling calico kitten. "She's the sweetest thing," he said. He handed her to me and headed home before I could gather the wits to object.

The cat had countless ticks, ear mites, fleas, worms—all the usual ailments of a stray. My daughter and I bathed her and cared for her, and within forty-eight hours the kitten transformed from a scared sickly thing to a merciless sprite. My seven-year-old was delighted, feeling the satisfaction of loving something back to health. My three-year-old was overjoyed to find something slow enough for him to catch. And my husband's blood pressure dropped when he finally paused long enough to hold the sleeping kitten in his lap.

Lord, give me courage when the unexpected arrives, and the wisdom to recognize the wonders I might find at my door.

June 5

> He had been eight years upon a project for extracting
> sunbeams out of cucumbers, which were to be put in
> phials hermetically sealed, and let out to warm the air in
> raw inclement summers.
> —Jonathan Swift, *Gulliver's Travels*

Caryll Houselander, English artist, writer, and mystic, believed the best way to benefit humanity was to make faces at people on the bus. Really crazy faces, she said. Such an unexpected lapse of decorum, I imagine, is like opening Swift's hermetically sealed phials of sunshine on a dreary summer day.

At the age of four my daughter insisted on wearing her princess costumes and bright yellow wellies. I tried to convince her to wear something more suitable. Then I noticed the people around us smiling, at the grocery store, the doctor's office. My girl was a break in the monotony, a beam of sunshine on a dreary day. I began to see her outrageous costumes as small acts of public service.

*Lord, help me to approach my dullest days with the ingenuity
of a child—and a sense of humor.*

June 6

> It has been a thousand times observed, and I must observe it once more, that the hours we pass with happy prospects in view are more pleasing than those crowned with fruition.
> —Oliver Goldsmith

In early June my daughter and I began to check the wild blackberry vines along the country lanes near our rural home. On our daily walks, she performed a thorough examination, waiting impatiently for the hard green knots of fruit to ripen to deep purple.

On the first truly hot day of summer, we stood on the gravel path, poking at the brambles with a stick. She found exactly one berry. She plucked it from the vine and examined it. She declared it a perfect specimen.

"I don't like blackberries," she said, handing it to me with a shrug. The happy prospect of those berries—and then their fruition—had been enough.

Lord, I can't help wondering what tomorrow will bring. Too often my wonder turns to anxiety and then fear, rather than hopeful anticipation. Today, let me treasure my good dreams of what is to come.

June 7

At morn—at noon—at twilight dim—
Maria! Thou has heard my hymn!
In joy and wo—in good and ill—
Mother of God, be with me still!
When the Hours flew brightly by
And not a cloud obscured the sky,
My soul, lest it should truant be,
Thy grace did guide to thine and thee;
Now when storms of Fate o'ercast
Darkly my Present and my Past,
Let my future radiant shine
With sweet hopes of thee and thine!
—Edgar Allan Poe, "Catholic Hymn"

Poe was inspired to write this poem when he heard the Angelus bells of a Catholic church ringing at six in the morning, then noon, then six in the evening. They were a call to prayer and meditation on the Mystery of the Incarnation—the moment when the angel Gabriel appeared to Mary and told her she would bear a son. The poem's speaker finds comfort in the regular peals of those bells, knowing that the loving care of the divine mother is as reliable as their ringing.

I love the thought of the troubled Poe taking comfort in those bells, which more than the passing of time, spoke to him of a love that endures the seasons for eternity.

Pray the Angelus today.

June 8

When [Jesus] had finished speaking, he said to Simon,
"Put out into the deep water and let down your nets for a
catch." Simon answered, "Master, we have worked all
night long but have caught nothing. Yet if you say so, I
will let down the nets." When they had done this, they
caught so many fish that their nets were beginning
to break.
—Luke 5:4–6

When Jesus approached, the fishermen had given up on
their task and were washing their empty nets. They'd
worked all night. They were tired, frustrated, and
disappointed. I'm sure the last thing Peter wanted was to
get back in that boat and row out to the deep waters to cast
the nets he had just cleaned.

"Master, we have worked all night long but have caught
nothing!" It's the lament of the frustrated soul.

"Yet if you say so, I will let down the nets," he then
says. Peter complains but then obeys. He casts the nets one
more time, and makes an abundant catch.

*Lord, give me the wisdom to know when to persist, especially
when I'm tempted to see my efforts as wasteful or foolish. Let
me know when it's time to clean the net, and when I should
row out into the deep.*

June 9

In winter I get up at night
And dress by yellow candle-light.
In summer, quite the other way,
I have to go to bed by day.
—Robert Louis Stevenson, "Bed in Summer"

My kids have never been easy sleepers. Even when they go to bed late, they rise at the first light of dawn. We installed shades and curtains in their bedroom, but they spring out of bed to greet the new day, no matter how dark we make their room. And good luck getting them to bed while the summer sun is still shining.

The church, too, appreciates the ebb and flow of the seasons, and the way our bodies respond. The liturgical year anticipates our need to feast and to fast, to rejoice and to mourn. Stevenson's poem reminds me in particular of the ancient tradition of the Lord of Misrule, a carnival game of reversal. A peasant might be crowned a king, or a child made the head of the family.

Summer can feel like one long carnival, when even the sun breaks the rules.

Let the kids stay up late. But only if they'll let you sleep in.

June 10

"Friends, why are you doing this? We are mortals just like you, and we bring you good news, that you should turn from these worthless things to the living God, who made the heaven and the earth and the sea and all that is in them. . . . [Y]et he has not left himself without a witness in doing good—giving you rains from heaven and fruitful seasons, and filling you with food and your hearts with joy."
—Acts of the Apostles 14:15–17

The crowds have just witnessed a miracle and heard the revelation of Christ. They've also received rains from the heavens, fruitful seasons, and abundant food—miracles in themselves. But instead of falling to their knees to worship God, they rush to crown Paul and Barnabas as Mercury and Jupiter. Imagine the apostles' frustration.

"We are mortals just like you!" they insist. Even when the choice is between being worshipped as a god or being killed, the apostles practice perfect humility and give all the glory to God.

Through whom or what is God working this summer to bring you his abundance and fill your heart with joy?

June 11

Let all guests who arrive be received as Christ.
—Rule of Benedict 53:1

In the summer we tend to have a lot of houseguests. Often these guests are unexpected. At least by me. My husband will run into someone and invite them back to our house for dinner—and forget to tell me.

Sometimes we don't have enough food, and I'm embarrassed. Sometimes we have plenty, but I still wish I could have done better: taken the laundry off the dining table, lit a scented candle, or at least washed my face.

In my more gracious moments, I see his hospitality not as a lack of consideration for me, but as a charism, his particular way of ministering to others. I think of St. Benedict's words and try to welcome our guests as Christ. If my husband met Christ on the road walking home from work, would I worry that my laundry isn't done? Would I eat less to offer him more?

Do you have a friend or houseguest due soon? Treat him or her with some portion of the hospitality you'd offer Christ.

June 12

As down in the sunless retreats of the ocean,
sweet flowers are springing no mortal can see,
so deep in my soul the still prayer of devotion,
unheard by the world, rises silent to thee.
—Thomas Moore, "As Down in the Sunless Retreats"

"Are these guys supposed to be in your yard?" our guest called out from the dining room. I was carrying dinner dishes to the sink when he saw, through the window, four men dressed in white from head to toe, carrying nets and cameras.

They were researchers from Shizuoka University in Japan, and they'd traveled all the way to rural Virginia to study the Brood II Cicadas. They took us on a tour of our own backyard, pointing out where the insects had tunneled out of the earth, clung to nearby vegetation, and molted into adulthood at last.

For seventeen years those cicadas were silent in the earth, unseen and unheard. But for a few weeks in June they lived in the light and sang for their mates.

Lord, as you know the depths of the earth and the sunless retreats of the ocean, you know me. The vastness of creation speaks to me of the depths of your care.

June 13

Lets in new light through the chinks that Time has made.
—Edmund Waller, "Of the Last Verses in the Book"

After four pregnancies, two miscarriages, six total years of nursing infants, and a major surgery, my body feels like a battered cottage. I used to fantasize that I would age gracefully and be a model of wisdom and maturity for my children. But it helps to remember the story my battered body tells.

I see the scar on my stomach, and remember my son's birth. The spots and freckles on my hands and arms speak of long days playing in the southern sun. The lines around my eyes crept in while I laughed, or cried. The gray hairs appeared after sleepless nights comforting a scared or restless child.

My body shows the wear of time. But my soul grows stronger with age.

Lord, may my spirit grow in strength and vigor even as my body ages.

June 14

Blessed are those who trust in the LORD
whose trust is the LORD.
They shall be like a tree planted by water
sending out its roots by the stream.
It shall not fear when heat comes,
and its leaves shall stay green;
in the year of drought it is not anxious,
and it does not cease to bear fruit.
—Jeremiah 17:7–8

We are not striving to be like trees: we *are* like trees.

This passage from Jeremiah gives us a sense of God's perfect design for us. God gives us all we need to fulfill our purpose: the thirst and the Living Water. He gives us the nourishment to grow and bear fruit. It's only when we turn away from God that we wither.

Today or tomorrow, find time to sit outside with a tree. Spend time looking closely. Be mindful of what you might learn from it.

June 15

I am only a mortal.
—Acts of the Apostles 10:26

As far as unlikely heroes go, Peter has always been my favorite. He had a temper. In the Gospels he's the one saying the wrong thing at the wrong time, questioning and even arguing with Jesus, and finally, denying him during the Passion. Three times!

But in the book of Acts we see what Jesus always saw in Peter—the rock. He is strong, brave, and fiercely loyal. And he's humble. When Cornelius falls at his feet in reverence, Peter tells him to get up. He's only mortal.

Such a towering figure in the church, St. Peter, who holds the very keys to the kingdom, and yet, he's only a man.

Lord, you know my strengths, and you see all I am capable of becoming. Be my encouragement when I feel my tasks are beyond my wisdom or my strength. Nothing is impossible for you.

June 16

No great thing is created suddenly, any more than a
bunch of grapes or a fig. If you tell me that you desire a
fig, I answer you that there must be time. Let it first
blossom, then bear fruit, then ripen.
—Epictetus

In one of my favorite children's stories, a Frog and a Toad
set about planting a garden. When the surly Toad's seeds
don't immediately sprout, he berates them. The
more-affable Frog warns that he'll scare the seeds to death,
so Toad plays them classical music and reads them stories.
While Toad busily finds new and inventive ways to
comfort his seeds and coax them from the earth, time
passes and the garden grows.

I'm too much like Toad: impatient, restless, and
desperate to know how it will all turn out. But there is no
way to rush progress. Growth and maturity take time, and
"above all," as the Jesuit prayer goes, we must "trust in the
slow work of God."

God, as gardens reach their fullness in the long days of
summer, I trust that you are slowly transforming me, too.

June 17

My book . . . is the nature of created things, and any time
I wish to read the words of God, the book is before me.
—St. Anthony of the Desert

I often hide from prayer in books. Even Scripture can be a distraction. I use a study Bible that encourages my terrible habit of diving down rabbit holes to mull over various translations of ancient words, to consider the debate over authorship of the Gospels, or to cross-reference the Old Testament with the New. I used to try to pass this off as *lectio divina*—holy reading. But it isn't really prayer. It's research.

I've spent much time trying to pin God down, figure God out. I search in vain for answers our creator has chosen to keep hidden. Today I will be more like St. Anthony. I will put the books away and read the words of God in the world around me.

Spend time today with a story in one of the Gospels. Read it more than once and imagine the story unfolding as if you were a character within it. Fill in the details the story doesn't provide.

June 18

Ill weede growth fast.
—John Heywood

We inherited six different flower gardens when we bought our home, more than I could ever tend. I've been shocked by how quickly the weeds grow, tall and hardy and impossible to pull out by the roots. The Bermuda grass is the worst—creeping low to the ground to cover dozens of feet in a matter of weeks. It's not just unsightly; its roots emit a chemical that harms the other plants. I couldn't keep up, even if I tried.

I consulted a professional. Her answer was to overfill the gardens with the good stuff. Choose my favorite perennials and ground covers, and propagate them until they filled the beds, leaving no room for the bad things to grow. Can we guard our souls in the same way?

What good fruit can you plant to overabundance in your soul's soil?

114

June 19

For day and night your hand was heavy upon me;
my strength was dried up as by the heat of summer.
—Psalm 32:4

When I taught my daughter the Ten Commandments, I was shocked to realize I break almost all of them on a daily basis. I say I worship only one God, but do I ever treat people or events or things as more important than that worship? I might not be a murderer, but do I harm others verbally or emotionally? Do I gossip and manipulate? I haven't coveted my neighbor's spouse, but have I neglected my own, or measured him unfairly against another?

In Psalm 32, David acknowledges his sin before the Lord, and praises God for his mercy, forgiveness, and unfailing love. What begins as a dirge ends with a joyful whoop. A psalm of penance becomes a psalm of gratitude.

Are you feeling weighed down, exhausted, uneasy with the world? Perhaps it's time for a thorough examination of conscience. Admit your faults and praise God joyfully!

June 20

Ants are creatures of little strength,
yet they store up their food in summer.
—Proverbs 30:25, *New International Version* translation

In the book *Frederick* by Leo Lionni, a family of mice is busy preparing for winter, gathering corn and nuts, wheat and straw. All except Frederick. All he does is daydream—staring at the colors in the meadow and studying the light of the sun.

When the family has eaten through winter's stores and exhausted their conversations, it's Frederick who saves them from the cold and drear. Frederick, who studied the sun, helps them to imagine again its warmth.

Maybe you aren't a gardener or farmer or artist, but you can still store up provisions for the lean times. Take time today to recall happy moments. Note their scent, feel, and taste. Store the memories to feed your spirit.

June 21

Why, this is very midsummer madness.
—Shakespeare, *Twelfth Night*

To ancient peoples, the summer solstice was seen as a day of "madness"—of supernatural possibility—to be celebrated with feasts and fire. Bonfires on hilltops on Midsummer's Eve were believed to have curative powers and to ward off evil spirits.

The church placed the nativity of St. John the Baptist on Midsummer's Eve—exactly six months before we celebrate the birth of his cousin Jesus, during that other great feast of light, Christmas, the winter solstice. And so we get a little bit of advent in the height of summer.

We often hear that the church adopted and Christianized pagan customs, smoothing out the rough ways. But C. S. Lewis, among others, argues that these primal celebrations and festivals somehow anticipated and longed for Christianity. Those early bonfires expressed our yearning to be fed, cured, protected, and saved by the light. Before the coming of Christ and John, the very seasons whispered the story of our salvation.

God sent John that we might recognize the light of salvation when it arrived. Make way for a little advent tonight and light a candle for St. John's birth.

June 22

God, after all, has given every substance in the world to
them . . . seed and earth and seas and stars.
—Caryll Houselander

My daughter picks up a dozen rocks a day on the road
by our house. Not special, beautiful rocks, but common
pebbles. She lines them up on our windowsills and they
become works of art. My son collects sticks and fallen
tree limbs. A feather or a piece of beach glass is a treasure
to them.

The art critic John Berger once imagined heaven as
invisible but close; we might find it, he mused, by simply
picking up the saltshaker. The small and unremarkable are
transformed in an instant by this God who is both infinite
and near, vast and small enough to fit in a palm, in a wafer
of bread.

Hunt for one small treasure as you go about your day.

June 23

The summer day was spoiled with fitful storm;
At night the wind died and the soft rain dropped;
With lulling murmur, and the air was warm,
And all the tumult and the trouble stopped.
—Celia Thaxter, "The Nestling Swallows"

St. Benedict was a twin. His sister, Scholastica, is also a saint, and there is a charming story of their last meeting on this earth. After spending the day together in "holy talk," Scholastica begged Benedict to stay the night. He refused, insisting he honor his own Rule by not spending a night away from his monastery. Scholastica—sensing this would be the last time she saw her brother—wept and prayed God would intercede. Within moments a sudden, violent storm made it impossible for him to leave.

"May Almighty God forgive you for what you have done," said Benedict reproachfully.

"I asked a favor of you, and you refused it," she replied. "I asked it of God, and He has granted it!"

St. Benedict, pray that I may never grow so rigid and habitual that I won't break my own rules for the sake of another.

June 24

My little sisters the birds, ye owe much to God, your
Creator, and ye ought to sing his praise at all times and in
all places. . . . Beware, my little sisters, of the sin of
ingratitude, and study always to give praise to God.
—St. Francis of Assisi

Our window unit air conditioners run almost constantly
during the Virginia summer. But in the evening, as the
sun sinks, the air cools enough for us to shut them off for
a while, to open the windows and hear the birds chatter
and sing.

Legend tells us that after hearing the preaching of
St. Francis, the birds bowed their heads and flew off to the
four corners of the earth to evangelize throughout creation.
I imagine the burst of song I hear on a hot summer night as
the prayer of thanksgiving that St. Francis gave them long
ago. They are thanking God for food and for flight, for
the day and all it brought, for the fountains and rivers that
quench thirst, the mountains and valleys that are refuge.
Our little sisters, singing the words of a saint, school us in
God's abundant love for all creation.

*Open the windows this evening and listen to the preaching of
the birds.*

June 25

I seek you,
my soul thirsts for you;
my flesh faints for you,
as in a dry and weary land where there is no water.
—Psalm 63:1

I was on a long walk with a friend in the heat of midday. We walked quickly, talking fast and covering more ground than I'd intended. Suddenly her voice grew distant. Conversation became impossible; I didn't understand. My vision went dim and blurry. She seemed far away, though she was walking right next to me. I wondered where we were. I stopped and reached out for her to brace myself. It turns out I was severely dehydrated. My brain and body were folding up.

Spiritual dryness can have similar effects—the soul thirsts and the flesh faints. We might feel exhausted, lost, and confused. God seems impossibly distant, and we are unable to see or feel his presence. The ancient prayers of the church, the liturgy, and the sacraments can help to replenish us. These sources never run dry.

Lord, when my soul thirsts and wilts, lead me to places where I can rest in your shadow and drink from your fountain.

SUMMER

June 26

I know what it is to have little, and I know what it is to
have plenty. In any and all circumstances I have learned
the secret of being well-fed and of going hungry, of
having plenty and of being in need. I can do all things
through him who strengthens me.
—Philippians 4:12–13

Last summer a historic storm knocked out power in our
area for ten days. We learned the hard way the value of
preparedness. In days of 100-degree temperatures and in
the dark nights that followed, those who had batteries,
working flashlights, water, and above all, ice, were
suddenly rich as kings.

We'd be wise to prepare as well for storms of the soul.
Paul says we need not be tempest-tossed by the vicissitudes
of life. This is not the pride of a stoic. Paul's steadfastness
is humble; he knows he depends on God.

*Lord, stay close, and keep me steady through all the wild
swings of weather and fortune.*

June 27

If Nature had been comfortable, mankind would never have invented architecture.
—Oscar Wilde

In the foothills of the Blue Ridge Mountains, housekeeping in the summertime is a losing battle. The parched earth coughs up clouds of red dust. It clings to our clothes and furniture. Sudden violent thunderstorms whip through the tall trees and cast countless limbs and brush into our yard. I spend hours picking up sticks, scrubbing floors and baseboards, sweeping cobwebs out of corners. I want to prove I'm in control. But it only takes a few minutes for nature to reassert her authority.

Many people feel close to God in nature, but the extremes of creation can make us feel small and insignificant. Sometimes, just staring into the mist of the Blue Ridge makes any personal connection with God seem as impossible as keeping my house clean.

Take a day to let some responsibility go. Do what needs to be done, but find an opportunity to let one of the more futile struggles go for the day.

June 28

Oh, somewhere in this favored land the sun is
shining bright;
The band is playing somewhere, and somewhere hearts
are light,
And somewhere men are laughing, and somewhere
children shout;
But there is no joy in Mudville—mighty Casey has
struck out.
—Ernest Lawrence Thayer, "Casey at the Bat"

My daughter, though she's only seven, has already declared her intention of becoming a writer. But when I told her about a summer writing contest for children, she responded, "What if I don't win?"

Her honesty took me by surprise. Many of us have hidden our lights under bushels for this same reason, but we usually aren't as honest about our motivations. My daughter isn't old enough yet to be too proud to reveal her fear of failure.

Pope Francis, speaking to a group of school-aged children, said we mustn't be afraid to fail—in life or in faith. "In the art of falling," he said, "what is important isn't not falling, but not remaining down."

When I "strike out" in life, Lord, as I surely will, give me the fortitude to stay in the game.

June 29

O, Spirit of the Summertime!
Bring back the roses to the dells;
The swallow from her distant clime,
The honey-bee from drowsy cells.

Bring back the friendship of the sun;
The gilded evenings, calm and late,
When merry children homeward run,
And peeping stars bid lovers wait.

Bring back the singing; and the scent
Of meadowlands at dewy prime;
Oh, bring again my heart's content,
Thou Spirit of the Summertime.
—William Allingham, "Song"

The yearning of all great fairy tales, J. R. R. Tolkien pointed out, is the desire to escape this world and regain something that we sense deep in our hearts was lost long ago. In fairy tales we are no longer at odds with nature; we talk to animals and hold counsel with trees.

Tolkien thought the Christian story was the best of all. In it we find the ultimate victory over death. We are returned at last to our lost love, God, who is our heart's content.

Read a fairy tale today. What lessons might it teach your older self?

June 30

Something there is that doesn't love a wall,
That sends the frozen-ground-swell under it,
And spills the upper boulders in the sun;
And makes gaps even two can pass abreast.
—Robert Frost, "Mending Wall"

We build walls around ourselves, often unintentionally. We distance ourselves from others, afraid of becoming dependent, or depended upon. "We keep the wall between us as we go," the poet later says.

God knows better what we need and acts as a wall-breaker. Over time, the freezing and thawing of the earth cracks and buckles the builder's work, and "makes gaps that even two can pass abreast." His will isn't accomplished all at once but through seasons of small pushes and pulls.

Have you built walls that are keeping you at a distance from your neighbors? Or do you need some space and time? Spend some time mending, or breaking down, your fences.

July 1

A garden requires patient labor and attention. Plants do not grow merely to satisfy ambitions or to fulfill good intentions. They thrive because someone expended effort on them.
—Liberty Hyde Bailey

My mother-in-law taught me to pinch back my mums until the Fourth of July. I am a terrible gardener, with no patience for labor or attention. I start out with good intentions, but by July my beds are hopelessly overgrown and thick with weeds. All but the mums. Those I obediently pinch back, remembering her words.

I remember her shaking her head at me for tossing a couple of pots of spent mums in the trash. "You should put those in the ground," she said. I looked at their brittle brown stalks skeptically. "Oh, you'd be surprised," she said. "They'll come back." She was right. They bloomed again. Now I never toss mums. My gardens are full of her advice.

She was born in July. Just today, I found a mum that I missed, heavy with newly formed buds. Another derelict survivor saved by her words.

Plant something in memory of someone you love. If you're anything like me, it will motivate you to care for your garden.

July 2

For the man sound in body and serene of mind there is
no such thing as bad weather; every sky has its beauty,
and storms which whip the blood do but make it pulse
more vigorously.
—George Gissing

As I write this, we are thirty inches above our typical summer rainfall. We've lived two weeks without the sun. The days have been so dreary I was tempted to light a fire in the fireplace—unthinkable in July in Virginia, especially in an old cottage with no air conditioning.

After days of board games and movies, I give up. We pull on our wellies and squish through the yard, slide in the wet red clay. The grass is deep green and knee-high; it's been too wet to mow. The weeds in the garden beds are taller than the children. The air is thick and heavy. Gnats hover near us in dark clouds. Bunnies and deer are feasting in the high grasses, and the birds are chattering and singing in the trees. A red fox and her cubs stop to stare in the neighbor's yard. The earth is drinking deep, overflowing, spilling out, pulsing with life.

There is no such thing as bad weather.

Lord, my moods are so dependent on the weather. Open my eyes to each day's beauty.

July 3

The hollow sea-shell, which for years hath stood
On dusty shelves, when held against the ear
Proclaims its stormy parents; and we hear
The faint, far murmur of the breaking flood.
We hear the sea. The Sea? It is the blood
In our own veins, impetuous and near.
—Eugene Lee-Hamilton, "Sea-Shell Murmurs"

When I was a kid we went every summer to Pensacola, Florida, for our beach vacation. I'd beg my parents to buy the biggest shell I could find in the souvenir shop. I was astonished that an object in a store filled with so much plastic and neon and airbrush paint could speak so insistently of the sea. No matter how long it sits on a dusty shelf, when we press it to our ears, a shell will tell us of its "stormy parent."

Of course, it's not really the sea we hear in the shell. Like Eugene Lee-Hamilton, they say it's only the blood pulsing in our veins or the ambient noise of the space around us, resonating within the shell's empty chamber. Cash registers, a clacking keyboard, honking horns, human breath and pulse—the whole mess of daily life that we've trained our ears to ignore—all drawn in and transformed to the voice of the sea.

Stop once in a while today and really listen to your world. What do you hear?

July 4

But a lifetime of happiness! No man alive could bear it: it
would be hell on earth.
—George Bernard Shaw, *Man and Superman*

Psalm 16 promises that we'll experience the "fullness of joy" and "pleasures forevermore" when we come into God's presence. Maybe that's why I've always been troubled by the thought that eternity will be boring. I imagine those endless summer days of childhood, when I grew tired of leisure and wanted to go back to school.

Why do I sometimes equate the "perfect happiness" God promises with boredom or leisure? The happiest times of my life have been a culmination of intense labor, risky leaps of faith, and even long periods of fear, sorrow, and worry.

G. K. Chesterton, Catholic apologist and George Bernard Shaw's intellectual sparring partner, insisted that real happiness is never "flat and round." It is the sum of all our experience, of joy and grief, of triumphs and losses—a "perilous balance," like a "desperate romance."

Reflect on a moment or a season of life when you felt really happy. I bet it wasn't flat or round. How would you describe it?

July 5

No man is an island, entire of itself.
—John Donne

In *The Little Island* by Margaret Wise Brown, a kitten comes to an island on a summer picnic and wants to know how this land is a part of the world. A fish tells the kitten a secret: all land is one land under the sea.

When I read this book to my children I think of John Donne's meditation on the ringing of church bells, of which the phrase "No man is an island" is a famous excerpt. Donne—like the fish—is letting us in on a secret: underneath all of creation, we are connected in Christ.

Lord, when I feel lonely and isolated and yearn for connection, remind me that I am part of what you have made whole.

July 6

Good is a good doctor, but Bad is sometimes a better.
—Ralph Waldo Emerson, *Conduct of Life*

At eleven years old, Maria Goretti, whose feast day is July 6, is one of the youngest canonized saints. Briefly: Maria was innocent and pure, but looked mature and beautiful, and her lusty neighbor Alessandro, little more than a boy himself, murdered her when she resisted his advances.

Alessandro spent the next thirty years of his life in prison. One night, he saw a vision of Maria gathering lilies in a garden. She approached him with the flowers, a symbol of her innocence. As he took them from her hands, each blossom burst into white flames. He soon begged forgiveness for Maria's murder. He even joined a Capuchin monastery as a lay brother, where he worked in the garden.

Devotion to Maria usually focuses on her purity. But what I really love about this story is that she and God don't give up on Alessandro. Ultimately, her death helps to bring about his salvation.

Lord of Mercy, you will never give up on me. Your goodness is more powerful than my worst sin.

July 7

> But one doesn't expect to get out of life what one has already learned that it cannot give, but rather one begins to see more and more clearly that life is only a kind of sowing time, and the harvest is not here.
> —Vincent van Gogh

We have moved four times in the last five years. At each house I've planted a small garden, and each year, we've moved before it flourished. Still, it pleases me to think of others enjoying the fruits of my labors. Recently I drove by our old house. The small pot of bee balm I'd planted in an empty bed had flourished to form a magnificent border.

We spend youth—our spring—anticipating the time when we will realize our dreams. But in adulthood we learn the hard lesson of fruition. Some dreams wilt in the summer heat of responsibilities, burdens, and trials. Some rewards will only be reaped by others. And sometimes we become so preoccupied with the work of life that we don't realize how much we've already achieved.

Be joyful in your work today. We often go on autopilot when we work. Try to be present and aware as you work. Find the joy in your labor.

July 8

If we accept Heaven we shall not be able to retain even
the smallest and most intimate souvenirs of Hell.
—C. S. Lewis, *The Great Divorce*

On that first truly hot day of the year, I feel compelled to
rid my house of clutter. The heat and humidity conspire
to make all my family's possessions seem too many and
too close. So many things seem unnecessary burdens. Why
have we been holding on to this stuff?

My soul, too, is cluttered with regrets, disappointments,
grudges, anger. These "souvenirs" might only bring me
pain, yet they can be hard to part with. They keep me
tethered to the past and afraid to go forward.

"Remember Lot's wife," Jesus tells us in the Gospels.
Her salvation lay before her. And yet she couldn't resist
looking back.

*Lord, what souvenirs of hell do I need to let go of? Help me to
release them so I may accept the heaven you offer.*

July 9

Do not look With horror on me,
but in kind compassion
Pity a wretch deserted and forlorn
In this sad place.
—Sophocles, *Philoctetes*

We were preparing to leave for the beach when our daughter discovered that our kitten had a bad wound on her leg, gaping and red. But the vet didn't even give her a bandage. In the wild, he said, this sort of thing would heal on its own. Except our kitten doesn't live in the wild. Afterward, we squirmed, cringed, or hurried out whenever she limped into the room.

My husband told the story of Philoctetes, the master archer with a leg wound so nasty his friends abandoned him on an island while he slept. For years he lived alone, his pain increased by his loneliness, until his countrymen realized they needed his bow to win the Trojan War.

Our kitten had no skill to offer. She had nothing but her cuteness, sadly diminished. It's easy to love something cute. But real love never fails.

Lord, give me the fortitude to love those you have committed to my care, no matter what.

July 10

We know that all things work together for good for those
who love God, who are called according to his purpose.
—Romans 8:28

We have way more yard than we can handle. Our grass has
gotten so long our neighbor offered to mow it for us.

We've also had more fireflies than usual. They flicker in
the dusk, flashing with some secret message. I watch them
from the window of the upstairs bedroom and listen to
the gentle breathing of my children in the dimness, sleep
overtaking them at the end of a hot day. I never tire of
this magic.

I wondered what was attracting them. It turns out our
unkempt grass is at least partly responsible. And the more
insects we draw to the yard, the healthier the grass will be.

I don't know what our overgrown lawn has to do with
loving God, except that even here I see evidence of our
creator's plans and purpose. And when I watch the fireflies,
I do love him a little more.

*Lord, you are the architect of all creation, but sometimes it's
easier to discern your patterns in nature than in my own life.
I know you have a plan for me. Let me know when it's okay
for me to let go, so you can do your work.*

July 11

The mind is its own place, and in itself
Can make a heaven of hell, a hell of heaven.
—John Milton, *Paradise Lost*

In an old folktale, Misery comes to stay with an old peasant couple. He makes their fire cold, their food bland, and he sleeps between them so they can't comfort each other.

One day, the wife realizes that their life wouldn't be so bad, if only they could drive Misery away. So they execute a plan to trap him deep in the woods. The fire burns brightly again, the food tastes good, and without Misery between them, the husband and wife keep each other warm at night.

I thought of this tale as we loaded up our car for the family vacation. Preparing to leave the house for a month with small children is stressful, and tensions were mounting. If I invite Misery to come with us to the beach, I realized, he most certainly will. But I can also decide to drive away and leave him behind.

Lord, help me to master my thoughts. Grant me the clear sight to recognize goodness in my life, unclouded by anxiety and worry.

July 12

Past are three summers since she first beheld
The ocean; all around the child await
Some exclamation of amazement here.
She coldly said, her long-lasht eyes abased,
Is this the mighty ocean? Is this all?
—Walter Savage Landor, "Gebir"

A road trip with children can make you feel trapped in one of Dante's circles of hell—the moaning, the whining, the mom-he's-touching-me's, the constant stops for bathroom breaks and snacks, the dashboard clock reminding you of your lack of progress. When we arrived after sixteen hours, it was past midnight, the ocean was black and invisible, and the children were fast asleep. We tucked them in and collapsed into bed, defeated.

The kids woke us at first light, and we all stumbled down the boardwalk bleary-eyed. For a moment I worried they'd be disappointed. Then I heard them gasp. A sudden break in the dunes had revealed the Atlantic and the sun rising above it. We were, all of us, stunned, literally stopped in our tracks. But just for a second. Then they ran for it.

When have you or your children been awed by natural beauty? Spend some time with the memory today.

July 13

Patience and tenacity of purpose are worth more than
twice their weight of cleverness.
—Thomas Henry Huxley, "On Medical Education"

At dusk, we stand on the beach, staring out at the water,
silently waiting. We are looking for the dark heads of
mother sea turtles. They crane out of the water, look to
shore, and disappear again. They are "staging," eyeing up
their nesting sites, and they will float and wait and float
some more—sometimes for hours—until it is safe to come
ashore and lay their eggs. For these endangered turtles the
stakes are very high. It's good that they're cautious.

For several days we have gone to the beach and waited
and watched. The mothers bob, waiting for the beach to
clear and for darkness to fall, while we try our best to be
still and quiet and unseen. But our best is not very good.
They are turtles, after all, ancient symbol of patience and
tenacity. We get hungry and the bugs start to bite. We pack
our bag and wander home.

Lord, create in me a patient heart.

July 14

> I see my way as birds their trackless way.
> I shall arrive,—what time, what circuit first,
> I ask not . . .
> He guides me and the bird.
> —Robert Browning, "Paracelsus"

In the morning the beach is pocked with shallow pits where mother turtles have laid their eggs in the night. My children have learned to spot the tracks of the newly hatched babies making their way from the nests to the ocean.

The turtles follow the light, and the brightest point on the beach is the horizon; their instincts lead them to the sea. The light pollution of overdeveloped coastlines is but one of many reasons the turtles are endangered. Even the light from a flashlight might distract a mother from protecting her nest or disorient a new hatchling. Their instincts betray them.

Our instincts don't always lead us to safety. For that, we rely entirely on God.

Lord, you are leading me, but I'm often distracted on my journey. When I take wrong turns, guide me back toward your light.

July 15

When despair for the world grows in me
and I wake in the night at the least sound
in fear of what my life and my children's lives may be,
I go and lie down where the wood drake
rests in his beauty on the water, and the great
heron feeds.
I come into the peace of wild things
who do not tax their lives with forethought
of grief. I come into the presence of still water.
And I feel above me the day-blind stars
waiting with their light. For a time
I rest in the grace of the world, and am free.
—Wendell Berry, "The Peace of Wild Things"

The Living Water. The Day Star. The Rock. The Branch. These are all names used to describe Christ in the Scriptures. God speaks to us in the natural world, using the language of nature to tell us who Jesus is.

As wild things find their rest in nature, we will only find our peace in Christ.

Make Berry's poem your prayer for today. When despair grows and you are afraid, you can rest in God, and for a time, come into the peace of wild things.

July 16

Ships that pass in the night and speak each other
in passing;
Only a signal shown and a distant voice in the darkness;
So on the ocean of life we pass and speak one another;
Only a look and a voice, then darkness again and
a silence.
—Henry Wadsworth Longfellow, *Tales of the Wayside Inn*

A "dark night of the soul" usually refers to doubts we encounter on the path to a mature relationship with God. Our human relationships can go through dark nights too. When our interactions become fleeting and perfunctory, we are like Longfellow's ships, sharing little more than a look and a voice.

Sometimes we've fallen into bad relationship habits—we don't call as much as we should, or we don't make time to reconnect. But there are also times when we simply must attend to the business of life, when our jobs or children require almost constant attention. Friendship or romance can seem like luxuries we can't afford, when we're just trying to make it through the day.

Lord, though at times we seem to be on different courses, you are drawing us in the same direction. Help us to grow in love for each other, and give us the patience and fortitude to outlast our dark nights.

July 17

Nae man can tether Time nor Tide.
—Robert Burns, "Tam O'Shanter"

I watch my daughter bodysurfing. She's a natural. She doesn't fear the breakers. She knows how to melt into a wave, how to let go. She judges in a second whether to duck, to float, or to let the water carry her to the shore. I spent hours as a child in the same way, playing in the ocean. But when I wade in to swim with her, I realize I've forgotten how to take the waves. I resist them, and they knock me down with such force that I'm disoriented, and my heart races with fear.

It takes time and practice to regain the trust of the child, to know when to swim out deeper and when to let go and let the waves carry us in.

Identify an area of your life where you move cautiously, uncertainly. What are you afraid of? What undermines your trust?

July 18

"Martha, Martha, you are worried and distracted by many things; there is need of only one thing. Mary has chosen the better part, which will not be taken away from her."
—Luke 10:41–42

My mother-in-law would sometimes start clearing the dinner dishes before we'd taken our last bite. We begged her to sit and linger at the table, to talk and rest—especially after a big holiday meal, one that she'd labored over for days. But it seemed almost painful for her to leave the work to someone else.

My mother-in-law was definitely a Martha. I always thought I was a Mary. Not anymore. Are any mothers of young children Marys? When you run a household, you begin to feel indispensable and even a little territorial.

Martha is important, but I really don't want to be Martha all the time. I want to remember to sit and listen to my husband, my children, my friends, our guests. It's often in the voices of others that we hear the voice of God.

Summer is the perfect time to practice being a little more like Mary. Leave a tedious chore for another day. Spend time in prayer or with your family.

July 19

A man is not idle because he is absorbed in thought.
There is a visible labor and there is an invisible labor.
—Victor Hugo, *Les Miserables*

My last pregnancy was complicated, and I spent a lot of time off my feet. Yet I remember it as a time of extreme inspiration and creativity. As a writer, I've never been more prolific. I've often wondered if those productive surges were hormonal, or even spiritual. But I think the answer is simpler. When I'm pregnant, I rest. I sleep. I eat right and take vitamins. I read more, and my brain seems to work better. When I'm not pregnant, all those activities seem like luxuries, the stuff of leisure.

But the idea of leisure as rest and relaxation is a very modern one. The ancients believed that leisure was its own important work—a time for the invisible labor of contemplation that is necessary for a spiritually fulfilling existence.

How do you spend your summer time? Make time for activities that clear your head and make you sharper and more productive—exercising, reading, or quiet prayer.

July 20

When I run, I feel His pleasure.
—Eric Liddell

Eric Liddell, the Scottish Olympian of *Chariots of Fire*
movie fame, was a devout Christian and a missionary. He
delayed a mission to China to run in the Olympics. He
said he believed that though God intended for him to go
to China, God also made him fast. "And when I run," he
said, "I feel His pleasure."

My friend, pastor Matt Gaventa, wrote a sermon
inspired by Liddell, in which he invited his congregation
to honor the Sabbath not merely by resting or going to
church or serving others, but by doing some activity that
is pleasing to God. It might look like work, he warned. It
might also look like play. It might be writing, or cooking,
or running fast. Whatever our particular talent, God is
honored when we use it. When we make our talent our
prayer, it gives him glory.

*Pay attention to those moments when you are doing your best
work. Delight in the pleasure that your talents give
your creator.*

July 21

Long have I loved what I behold,
The night that calms, the day that cheers;
The common growth of mother-earth
Suffices me—her tears, her mirth,
her humblest mirth and tears.
—William Wordsworth, *Peter Bell*

I've always loved to meditate on the first words of John 3:16—"For God so loved the world." I think we tend to skip to the end too quickly. Why did God give us his Son? Out of love for this world.

This excerpt from Wordsworth makes me imagine God delighting in the lilies of the field, in the flowering of all he created. He takes joy in our flowering too. And not just in our hard-won triumphs but also in our trivial victories, our common growth. He's moved by our humble, everyday failures, disappointments, and tears.

Lord, when I grow cynical and hard of heart, soften me with love for your creation.

July 22

When winds are raging o'er the upper ocean,
and billows wild contend with angry roar,
'Tis said, far down, beneath that wild commotion,
That peaceful stillness reigneth evermore.
—Harriet Beecher Stowe, "When Winds Are Raging"

Harriet Beecher Stowe is best known as the author of *Uncle Tom's Cabin*, the novel that, according to legend, prompted Abraham Lincoln to say when he met her in 1862, "So you're the little woman who wrote the book that started this great war."

It's hard to imagine any "peaceful stillness" reigning during the bloodiest conflict in American history. Yet, even Stowe, who lived through these horrors, believed that a greater, peaceful force governed all.

That peaceful force is Christ, who brings an end to chaos, death, and doubt. "Fear not," he says over the roar of the storm and the waves. "Have faith."

Lord, even in chaos and commotion, you are there. Gather us into your perfect stillness and give us peace.

July 23

For surely I know the plans I have for you, says the LORD,
plans for your welfare and not for harm, to give you a
future with hope.
—Jeremiah 29:11

During one of the darkest periods of my life, I met my
sister on the coast of Lake Michigan for a vacation. I spent
days submerged in grief. One day, I noticed a plaque over
the breakfast table in this beach cottage with these words
from Jeremiah.

For the first time in weeks, I felt my soul revive. I loved
the message—these were the exact words I needed to hear.
But I loved even more that it had been there all along,
unnoticed. I felt then the power of unseen prayers.

I wondered what the owners of our cottage had endured
that made these words a comfort. In my wonder I was
praying too, praying the words of an ancient prophet with
people I'd never met, clinging with all of them to the same
promise.

*Pray now for someone you don't know, someone you've never
met. Offer them this promise from Jeremiah, that the Lord
will give them a hope and a future.*

July 24

"Isn't God upon the ocean,
Just the same as on the land?"
—James Thomas Fields, "The Captain's Daughter"

St. Brendan was a sixth-century monk who spent much of his life on the ocean. He and his brothers were famous adventurers, and according to legend, they traveled all the way to America almost a thousand years before Columbus set sail. They were searching for paradise, but they ended up in West Virginia. A stone there bears ancient Irish writing that some say tells the story of Christ's birth.

Many people in Brendan's time thought the ocean was the end of the earth. But he knew that nothing in creation, or in our lives, is beyond God's sovereignty. The Lord's dominion extends to every corner. So Brendan set out into the vast Atlantic in a crude wooden boat. He sailed all the way to America to tell the story of the Incarnation to the stones.

Is there a part of your life that feels hopelessly unknown? God is there. When you feel lost, trust that he will help you to navigate, even in uncharted waters.

July 25

Backward, turn backward, O Time, in your flight,
Make me a child again, just for tonight!
—Elizabeth Akers Allen, "Rock Me to Sleep"

Summer doesn't have to be about exotic vacations or extreme adventure camps. Think of the simple pleasures of childhood: digging in the sand or dirt, splashing in the rain, catching fireflies in a jar, skipping stones across the water, eating outdoors on a blanket. None of these activities costs extra money or even vacation days. They require no travel and very little time. But they feed the senses.

We might approach our faith the same way. Have we wandered from the essentials? Are we exhausted by church politics or parish squabbles? Return to the first things this summer. Reconnect with the Jesus of the Gospels and the traditions that infused your childhood with mystery and meaning.

Get back to the basics this summer. Become like a child again—if only for a few moments—in your play and your faith.

July 26

God! God! With a child's voice I cry,
Weak, sad, confidingly—
God, God!
—Elizabeth Barrett Browning, "The Soul's Travelling"

Affliction can turn us into children again. Scripture, tradition, the stories of the saints, art, poetry, theology—all these are comforts for the healthy, mature heart. They might come to nothing for the one in agony, afraid in the night, buckling under the cross. Then, nothing is real but need, and the only relief is his name. God! God!

Lord, sometimes your name is the only prayer I can manage. I call out to you, like a child calling for her father in the night. Let me know you are near.

July 27

Gray hair is a crown of glory;
it is gained in a righteous life.
—Proverbs 16:31

Though they are never mentioned in the Gospels, legend and tradition tell us that Joachim and Anne were the parents of Mary. They were an older couple, childless for most of their lives, and their daughter's birth was an answer to their years of prayer.

Whatever their names, Jesus had grandparents, and this mere fact seems worth celebrating. It gives us another opportunity to wonder at the mystery of the Incarnation. Jesus was born into a human family, and his life was part of an ongoing story.

Knowing where we came from can help us to understand our lives. Grandparents connect us with the past and show that we are part of a bigger picture.

Make a note to call grandparents or grandchildren, or exercise some kindness to an elderly person you know.

July 28

I do not know what I may seem to the world, but as to myself, I seem to have been only like a boy playing on the sea-shore and diverting myself in now and then finding a smoother pebble or a prettier shell than ordinary.
—Sir Isaac Newton

It's not about me.

I've had to adopt this as my mantra lately. When you write for publication you get used to receiving unsolicited criticism and even outright personal attacks. I've offended people I meant to compliment. We read through the lens of our own experience, and often we interpret work in ways the author never intended, for better or worse.

Is this not true of so many of our misunderstandings in life? We ascribe intent to harm where there was none, only thoughtlessness or self-absorption. Or perhaps we're on the other side, and we've gotten so lost in wondering how we are perceived by others that we forget that they are just as worried about their self-image as we are.

This simple phrase—it's not about me—reminds me, when I feel wounded or angry, to consider the burdens of others, all the weight they carry.

Today, take a break from obsessing over how others see you. God sees you as his beloved child.

July 29

Little drops of water, little grains of sand,
Make the mighty ocean and the pleasant land.
So the little minutes, humble though they be,
Make the mighty ages of eternity.
—Julia Abigail Fletcher Carney, "Little Things"

From a hill near our house my children can watch for my husband as he walks home from work. We are usually outside then, feeding the horses or riding bikes on the paved parking lot of the barn across the street. We mark the seasons on that hill.

In spring, white blossoms float from the trees and hang suspended in the air around us. In summer, the afternoons are heavy with rain or the want of it. In autumn the maples are aflame with color, and fallen leaves crunch under our feet. In winter, he won't be home before dark.

The overwhelmingly big events of my life—the birth of children, my wedding day—have gone blurry in my memory. But not this humble moment, repeated every day and in every season. These are the moments we miss when we lose someone. And I hope they're the moments God restores to us in eternity.

Lord, thank you for those little moments and mundane rituals that give meaning and continuity to my days.

July 30

Dost thou love life? Then do not squander time; for that
is the stuff life is made of.
—Benjamin Franklin

We are trained to maximize our days. Doing one thing
well isn't good enough anymore; we have to multitask. In
such an atmosphere, sitting in silence before a monstrance
holding a consecrated host might seem not just arcane and
bizarre but like an extravagant waste of time.

And yet, St. Faustina said that the practice of adoring
the Eucharist is so pleasing to God that for every holy hour
we spend, he gives every man, woman, and child a special
grace. Outrageous, right?

If you love life, there is no better use for an hour.

*Find a holy hour near you. Squander your time,
but with God.*

July 31

Men are but children of a larger growth.
—John Dryden

I hate asking for help. The truth is, I don't like to be perceived as weak. I want to project an image of strength and independence. That's the praise I crave more than any other.

It's scary to admit how childlike we remain, even when we're grown, even when we have children of our own. The psalms tell us that God will comfort us as a mother, but on earth, his touch often comes to us through the hands of others. There's no shame in allowing them to be Christ for us.

Lord, in many ways I still feel like a child. Let me never be too proud to ask for help when I need it. Give me the sensitivity to know when you're asking me to be your hands for others.

August 1

Catch, then, o catch the transient hour;
Improve each moment as it flies.
Life's a short summer—man a flower;
He dies—alas! How soon he dies!
—Samuel Johnson, "Winter: An Ode"

In his seventy-five years, Samuel Johnson wrote poems, essays, criticism, and a dictionary. Yet he was plagued by fear that he wasn't getting enough done. His journals are almost comical in this regard. He is forever making new resolutions to get up earlier, to be more productive, to improve his health so he can do more work. He's constantly regretting that life is too short and that he hasn't accomplished more.

The resolutions might be the only thing I have in common with Dr. Johnson. I'm embarrassed by how many self-improvement schemes I've undertaken with fervor only to abandon them in forgetfulness, laziness, illness, or crisis.

And yet, it's good to desire reform. We shouldn't despair at our flaws, but neither should we accept them. We should never settle for less when we suspect we're capable of more.

Lord, grant me the resolve to reform, and when I fail, the humility to try again without despair.

August 2

Long is the way
And hard, that out of Hell leads up to light.
—John Milton, *Paradise Lost*

My mother died when I was fourteen. She was diagnosed with cancer in August and died a year later in September. Ever since, I've associated the dog days with bad news, and late summer has been a difficult time for me.

Sometimes I'm ashamed of my grief. It's been more than twenty years, I think. I should be over it by now. But I may never get over it. Her life and her loss shaped who I am, and will be among the burdens I carry to my grave. Time heals all wounds, they say. Maybe not this one.

But there is One who can heal what even time cannot.

The path of grief is long and hard, and we all grow weary at times. Spend time today meditating on an empty space in your life that still causes you sadness. Pray for healing.

August 3

Thou that to grapes and weeds and little wild flowers
givest so liberally,
Shed, shed thyself on mine and me, with but a fleeting
ray out of thy million millions,
Strike through these chants.

. . . Prepare my lengthening shadows,
Prepare my starry nights.
—Walt Whitman, "Thou Orb Aloft Full-Dazzling"

Whitman hungers for the sun, for a restorative power so great that even a fleeting ray would sustain him. God does not deal in portions. He gives liberally. His love is perfect, whole, and complete, and he sheds it on all. But we all have times of spiritual darkness. God is still there. But he seems far away and invisible.

Let us be the moon in someone's dark night. We may reflect but a fleeting ray of God's perfect light, but it can be enough to dispel the shadows.

Lord, shed your light on me, fuse thyself here, so that I may reflect your love to those I meet today.

August 4

Pale in her fading bowers the Summer stands,
Like a new Niobe with clasped hands,
Silent above the flowers, her children lost,
Slain by the arrows of early Frost.
—Richard Henry Stoddard, "Ode"

Niobe was the queen of grief from the ancient myths. All fourteen of her children were slain by the arrows of vengeful gods. Stoddard compares the fading summer to Niobe's loss, as flowers and color and warmth wane.

In August, summer's height, we celebrate the feast of the Assumption, the story of a new Niobe, a mother who stared death in the face and yet persisted in hope.

In Greek Orthodox icons of *The Dormition of Theotokos,* Mary's body sleeps on her funeral bier while Jesus stands over her, cradling her soul in his hand. Roman Catholics believe that Mary was assumed both body and soul. Either way, the claim is extravagant: victory over death isn't reserved for the divine. It's extended to all humanity.

Lord, let me see in summer's fading not the grief of loss but the promise of eternal life.

August 5

I will arise and go now, for always night and day
I hear lake water lapping with low sounds by the shore;
While I stand on the roadway, or on the pavements grey,
I hear it in the deep heart's core.
—William Butler Yeats, "The Lake Isle of Innisfree"

Yeats said that he was inspired to write this poem while standing on the Strand in London. He heard a tinkling of water from a tiny display in a shop window, an advertisement for cold drinks. Just this simple and mundane image, this soft sound on a busy London street, was enough to cast his memory back to his childhood at the lake.

The landscapes of our childhood can have that kind of power—even if the landscape we remember is only that of the family house. I still dream of the house I grew up in, an unremarkable brick and siding ranch like a million others built in the 1960s. But to me, it is the place of enduring comfort.

Lord, the heart's core always speaks of you. Draw me toward the home you made for me.

August 6

Life! We have been long together,
Through pleasant and through cloudy weather;
'Tis hard to part when friends are dear;
Perhaps 'twill cost a sigh, a tear;
Then steal away, give little warning,
Choose thine own time;
Say not Good night, but in some brighter clime
Bid me Good morning!
—Anna Laetitia Aikin Barbauld, "Life"

Summer is a time of upheaval in a college town. Students graduate and strike out on their own, and the undergrads leave until fall. Friends and colleagues work summer jobs in distant places, or travel home to be with their families, or take new jobs and move away for good. We seem all summer, every summer, to be saying good-bye.

I'll never be able to give my children what I had growing up—stable years with the same friends growing up together on the same streets, with grandparents, aunts, and uncles a short drive away. Instead, I teach them to take the parting hand with grace. As C. S. Lewis said, Christians never say good-bye. I teach my children to say, "See you later."

Lord, when I have to take my leave of those dearest to me, fill me with confidence that we will meet again—here or There.

August 7

Sound loves to revel near a summer night.
—Edgar Allan Poe, "Al Aaraaf"

In the long days of summer I often find myself outside at twilight, watching the kids play, their voices mingling with the chatter of the birds, the distant whir of a tractor making hay on the hillside, the neighbor's dog yapping, the clatter of a passing train. The sounds, as Poe poignantly puts it, "revel in a summer night," playing in the air. I close my eyes and listen to the music they make.

The line is from a long poem that describes a sort of purgatory where souls wait to be ushered into heaven. But it's not really a coherent story. It seems Poe had one primary goal in mind: to create something extravagantly beautiful through sound and rhythm. In those beautiful sounds, he heard the voice of the divine.

Go outside this evening and sit quietly. Listen to the song of a summer night on earth.

August 8

Time is like a river made up of the events which happen,
and a violent stream; for as soon as a thing has been
seen it is carried away, and another comes in its place,
and this will be carried away too.
—Marcus Aurelius, *The Meditations*

Resignation to the endless flow of time is a popular bit of
ancient wisdom. Think of Ecclesiastes: To everything there
is a season. The sun rises and sets. We plant and reap. We
accept that time is a flowing river of passing events, that
cannot be changed or influenced by humanity. All earthly
effort to the contrary is in vain.

But in the early church, the message is startlingly
different. In Ephesians, we are called to redeem the
time—not to submit but to work to transform our world
and make it better. We've come from darkness into the
light of Christ, who can do all things and restore all losses.
Even our lost time.

*Do you need to adjust your priorities? Are there commitments
or people you've been neglecting, or unproductive hobbies that
suck up too many hours? Make a plan to use your time
more wisely.*

August 9

Loud, a mid-summer and a mid-wood bird
Who makes the solid tree trunks sound again. . . .
The bird would cease and be as other birds
But that he knows in singing not to sing.
The question that he frames in all but words
Is what to make of a diminished thing.
—Robert Frost, "The Oven Bird"

Summer reaches its height and the world seems charged
with fertility, light, and abundance. Yet we sense the
coming of autumn. I stand under the canopy of our giant
poplars and count the leaves that drift from their branches
in the breeze. They are yellowing at the edges. My children
have grown older, taller, with new freckles and scars.
Summer is passing into memory.

What do we make of this? We sense a strange
disjunction with the earth, with its passing away. We
wonder at time and its passage, how it makes things old
and wears them out. We grow and change and die—we
know these to be facts. Yet sometimes it all feels wrong and
impossible. We know we were made for eternity.

*Today, take time to be still and listen and look. Search for the
sense of the eternal. Let that feeling give you confidence and
fill you with love.*

August 10

Keep up your courage, because not one of you
will be lost.
—Acts of the Apostles 27:22, *New International Version*
translation

Even in the worst episodes of human history we find
stories of heroic men and women who inspire the hopeless.
Just one person's faith can be the difference between life
and death.

There are times in life when we will need to be carried,
and there's no shame in that. That's why it's so important
to belong to a church, a community of believers who can
do the heavy lifting when we just don't have the strength.

Lord, I have relied so much on your church to carry me
through the storms of my life. Help me to grow strong in my
faith so that I, too, may be able to carry another.

August 11

He that lacks time to mourn, lacks time to mend.
Eternity mourns that. 'Tis an ill cure
For life's worst ills, to have no time to feel them.
Where sorrow's held intrusive and turned out,
There wisdom will not enter, nor true power, Nor aught
that dignifies humanity.
—Sir Henry Taylor, *Philip van Artevelde*

The Victorians knew how to mourn. They stopped the clocks, covered the mirrors in their homes with black cloth, wore black dresses or arm bands for months. I imagine it was comforting to have the outside world reflect what was felt within. The customs confirmed that our losses mattered, that the world had been altered, and that we needed time to drop out of society, time to mend.

In our time we grieve privately and without ceremony, if we have time to grieve at all. The world rushes right along just as it did before. But when wounds don't properly heal, they come open again. Grief becomes bitterness, rather than wisdom. We must always remember that God gives us everything we need to heal, if we'll stop and spend some time doing what must be done.

Lord, let me, by my actions, words, or presence, be a balm to one who is grieving.

168

August 12

Just before daybreak, Paul urged all of them to take some food, saying, "Today is the fourteenth day that you have been in suspense and remaining without food, having eaten nothing. Therefore I urge you to take some food, for it will help you survive; for none of you will lose a hair from your heads."
—Acts of the Apostles 27:33–34

After two weeks in a violent storm, the men on this ship are exhausted and hopeless. But Paul has a plan. He commands them to eat. He comforts them with the promises of scripture—not a hair on their heads will be lost. And then he tells them to get to work.

Paul's advice is both practical and mystical. God promises to see us through every storm, but we mustn't sit in despair and wait to be rescued. Acts of courage and leaps of faith require physical and spiritual strength. First, we must eat.

Write down Paul's plan for use during your next state of emergency: 1) Nourish your body with food and rest; 2) Feed your spirit with the sacraments and Scriptures; 3) Marshall all your skill and strength—and the strengths of those around you—to chart a course to safety; and 4) Trust God to do the rest.

August 13

I am in distress;
my eye wastes away from grief,
my soul and body also.
For my life is spent with sorrow,
and my years with sighing;
my strength fails because of my misery,
and my bones waste away.

I am the scorn of all my adversaries,
a horror to my neighbors,
an object of dread to my acquaintances;
those who see me in the street flee from me . . .

But I trust in you, O LORD.
—Psalm 31:9–11, 14

Well, tell us how you really feel, King David. This is an excellent example of what I call an adult temper tantrum. I have them all the time, so I was surprised and comforted to find how often they occur in Scripture—and not from the faithless either, but from those closest and dearest to God.

In Numbers, God overhears the people grumbling and strikes back with fire. So what's the difference between their complaints and David's?

David ends his tantrum with a simple prayer, saying essentially, *I trust in you.*

Go ahead: make a list of every complaint you have at this moment, no matter how trivial, and give it to God. But end with David's prayer: I trust in you.

August 14

For God alone my soul waits in silence.
—Psalm 62:1

One summer I spent three of my vacation days on a silent retreat at the Abbey of Gethsemani, a trappist monastery in Kentucky. I headed for the hills, basically, to keep my mouth shut for a weekend. On their website, I'd seen the monks entering the iron gates of their enclosure under the words "God alone," and thought, *This is exactly the vacation I need.*

It's good to recognize and celebrate the transcendent moments amidst the chaos of daily life. It's good to hear the voice of God in the voices of those we love, and to see his hand in all creation. But sometimes I crave what the monks of Gethsemani have: not God amidst, but God alone.

Turn off the television, the computer, and your phone, and sit in silence. Don't talk or pray; just listen. Even if only for a moment.

August 15

Sweet Memory! Wafted by the gentle gale,
Oft up the stream of Time I turn my sail.
—Samuel Rogers

In her autobiography, *A Circle of Quiet*, Madeleine L'Engle writes of *chronos* and *kairos*, the Greek words for time. Chronos is clock time. Kairos is the immeasurable moment, an intersection with eternity. God's time.

Rocking her grandchild, L'Engle felt no older than she had when she'd rocked his mother. She sang the same lullabies, whispered the same soothing words. And yet, she knew that chronos had done work. L'Engle says we need both words in moments like these, when we feel our temporal selves colliding with our eternal, essential selves in the stream of Time.

Each time we celebrate Mass we are lifted out of chronos and into kairos. We are in God's time, and we come to the table with all the angels and saints. But sometimes my eyes are too blind to see it.

Lord, when chronos wears me down, and I feel life passing too swiftly in the stream of time, help me to remember those moments when your time has broken through and I have been given a foretaste of eternity.

August 16

"The harvest is past, the summer has ended,
and we are not saved."
—Jeremiah 8:20

Scholars believe Jeremiah wrote these despairing words as the Chaldean invaders bore down on Israel, but he was speaking both literally and metaphorically. Harvest is a time for reaping what you've sown, and Israel is coming up empty-handed.

What a terrible cry of frustration and regret—the summer has ended, and we are not saved.

Summer, the season of hope and joy and freedom, is passing. I wake and find myself older, and realize my youth is behind me. It's time for the harvest. But what have I sown? Not nearly enough—not even to last one winter.

Lord, I'm not ready! I didn't prepare!

God, I thought I'd be more by now—more accomplished, more mature, more stable, just . . . more. Don't let me despair when I'm faced with all I haven't done. Help me to fulfill your plans for me.

August 17

It is well to lie fallow for a while.
—Martin Farquhar Tupper, "Of Recreation"

In traditional farming and gardening, fallow periods, when the soil is left tilled but unplanted, are seen as essential to the health and abundance of future crops.

When we're not producing as much as we'd like, our impulse is to work harder and longer and faster. We feel guilty about taking time off. But if you're feeling burnt out and depleted, it might be more productive in the long term simply to lie fallow for a while.

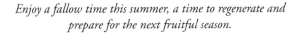

Enjoy a fallow time this summer, a time to regenerate and prepare for the next fruitful season.

August 18

O, I have suffered
With those that I saw suffer; a brave vessel,
Who had, no doubt, some noble creature in her,
Dashed all to pieces! O, the cry did knock
Against my very heart. Poor souls, they perished!
—William Shakespeare, *The Tempest*

In 1715 a hurricane sunk a fleet of Spanish ships off the coast of Florida. The survivors washed up near present-day Vero Beach. For years, archeologists have been diving down to the ocean floor and bringing back artifacts from the wrecked fleet. Some of these pieces are now housed in the McLarty Treasure Museum, where my husband took the kids on one rainy vacation day. He discovered among the displays of rusted nails and hand-carved pipes a collection of crucifixes, the largest no more than two inches long. Hundreds of years in the ocean had diminished them, and most long ago had lost the corpus, but some were still intact—Christ's small features, once minutely and lovingly crafted, erased.

We all have moments when we feel like castaways, lost and abandoned, and God seems distant and invisible. All we can do then is cling to the cross and hold on for dear life.

*Lord, do not hide your face from those who are suffering.
Comfort and strengthen each of us when our own
Passion comes.*

August 19

And he was transfigured before them, and his face shone like the sun, and his clothes became dazzling white.
—Matthew 17:2

Before the apostles see Jesus transfigured, his face radiant and his clothes dazzling, before they hear the voice of God revealing that this is his beloved son, they must climb. Mt. Tabor, which tradition names as the site of this mystery, rises abruptly from the surrounding level lands. I imagine it would have taken them at least a couple of days to reach the summit.

Did the apostles follow Jesus silently, humbly? Did they have complete and unfailing trust in where he was leading them? Or did they wonder if this was all really necessary, where they'd end up, and what would happen when they finally arrived? The Gospels don't tell us. But we know Peter was among them, and it's hard to imagine he didn't voice his concerns at some point.

When they reach their destination at last, they are "overcome by sleep," exhausted. This is when the miracle happens. They see, however briefly, who Christ really is—God's beloved Son—and who we will be in eternity, our resurrected bodies in the company of the saints and prophets.

Lord, when I am exhausted by the journey and the weight of my burdens, give me a glimpse of your face, a brief sight of your plan for me, so that I may find the strength to go on.

August 20

"Take nothing for your journey, no staff, nor bag, nor
bread, nor money—not even an extra tunic."
—Luke 9:3

Our house was so badly damaged by a summer storm
that we had to vacate it for two months while contractors
rebuilt the upstairs. We left with little more than the
clothes on our backs. I didn't even have an extra diaper for
the baby.

We were soon overwhelmed by the kindness of people
we barely knew. A colleague made sure we had a room in
the inn. A woman I sing with in choir saw the damage
and sought us out to offer us her carriage house. Knowing
we hadn't slept, a neighbor came to the inn, where—like
everyone for a 100-mile radius—we had no electricity, to
bring us iced coffee. Even some extra diapers appeared.

When we're self-sufficient, we're more likely to throw
up walls, to be exclusive. Jesus' instructions for the apostles
forced them to depend on the hospitality of others, to trust
that in the communities where they were going, they'd
build relationships, not walls.

*Make a list of how God has met your needs through someone
else. Ask God to show you how to reach out and share
what you have.*

August 21

I avoid looking forward or backward, and try to keep
looking upward.
—Charlotte Brontë

We were headed out the back gate on our evening walk
when my daughter bent over to tie her shoe. She was in a
fit about some perceived injustice, and mid-rant, she lost
her balance and fell flat on her back. This indignity was
the last straw, and she would have burst into tears. But at
just that moment, a large flock of geese soared overhead.
Look! I called to her. Look up! She looked up and she saw
them and smiled. In an instant she was drawn out of her
deep care and worry and restored to the world.

What would it mean to always look upward? To stop
fretting about what lies ahead or regretting what lies
behind? To forsake the usual order of things and fix our
eyes on heaven?

We are distracted by our cares and worries. We keep our
heads down and try to get through the day. But God is
always calling out, Look up! Look up!

*Lord, call me out of my self, keep me focused on you, so that I
may be more present to all that is good in the
present moment.*

August 22

For men may come and men may go,
But I go on forever.
—Alfred, Lord Tennyson, "The Brook"

Have you sat by a stream lately? The water babbles and slips and glances its way to join the brimming river, sometimes pulling life into its stream, or bearing life afloat on its course. But there is no life in the brook itself, no will but to follow its inevitable path forever.

For Tennyson, nature tells the divine story and speaks to our deepest longings for eternal care. But it is an imperfect and incomplete tale.

In Christ alone do we find the *living* eternal water—an eternal stream guided not by a blind will but by love.

God, thank you for nature's reminders of your everlasting love. When I am weary and worn out, help me to take a drink from your stream of life.

August 23

So fades a summer cloud away;
So sinks the gale when storms are o'er;
So gently shuts the eye of day;
So dies a wave along the shore.
—Anna Laetitia Aikin Barbauld, "The Death of the Virtuous"

In the first book of Kings, God warns Elijah that he's about to pass by. There is a great wind, but the Lord is not in it. There's an earthquake, but the Lord is not in it. Then there's a fire, but the Lord isn't there either. And after this great display of power and pyrotechnics, there is only "sheer silence."

We're waiting for God to speak to us in big ways, or to see, like Moses, our burning bush. But maybe God speaks as the seasons change, or as a cloud fades, or the gale sinks, or the sun sets, or a wave dies—gently, almost imperceptibly.

Sometimes we long to hear the voice of God directing us. But we should not think of silence as abandonment. Instead, remember Elijah, and listen for the still, small voice that guides.

What keeps you from listening for God's still small voice?
Resolve to cherish some silence in prayer today.

August 24

Stronger by weakness, wiser men become
As they draw near to their eternal home:
Leaving the old, both worlds at once they view
That stand upon the threshold of the new.
—Edmund Waller, "On the Divine Poems"

Sometimes we cross a threshold without notice. And then there are times when we know we are on the brink of permanent change: marriage, the birth of a child, a new home, a new career, retirement. We stand upon the threshold, with both worlds in view, feeling excitement and fear. We might find that we long to stay in the familiar past—even when it is less than perfect. We resist our new beginning.

Did Joshua linger at the threshold when, after the death of Moses, God commanded him to lead the people and cross the Jordan? "Be strong and courageous," commanded the Lord. "Do not be frightened or dismayed, for I am with you wherever you go."

*You have promised to stay with us, Lord, wherever we go.
Give me the courage to cross the thresholds in my life with
confidence and hope.*

August 25

Listen, I will tell you a mystery! We will not all die, but we
will all be changed.
—1 Corinthians 15:51

Summer is old and spent. It's time for autumn's crisp wind
and the unburdening of the branches, for a blanket of
snow to soothe the parched earth like the cold rag on a
child's fevered skin.

Yet we will mourn summer's passing, and the sleeping
of all that grows. And we are right to do so. "Perhaps the
wind wails so in winter," wrote George Eliot, "for what has
been and is not."

We sense that we were not created for this same fate.
Plants and flowers and animals may die, but not us, not
those we love. All the poets sing the same song down the
staircase of time: It cannot be!

*Lord, you have promised that we will not die. But we will be
changed. While the earth sleeps, let me remember that it is
gathering strength to leap forth in spring, a new creation.*

August 26

Letting go is seldom easy—whether it's letting go of our children, our parents, or our childhood feelings. But just as the root systems of plants often have to be divided for healthy growth to continue, the different generations within a family may have to pull apart for a while for each to find its own healthy identity.

—Mr. Rogers

I didn't leave the state of Louisiana until I was twenty-six years old, when I moved to Pittsburgh for graduate school. Where I come from, kids grow up to live around the corner from their parents. Even going to college an hour away was a bold statement of independence. Moving to north Louisiana was unheard of. But north of the Mason-Dixon? It just wasn't done.

The first few months in Pittsburgh I was sure I'd made a terrible mistake. I didn't know a soul. Even the landscape was alien: I'd never seen hills or snow. I hadn't been a practicing Catholic for years back in Louisiana, but when homesickness became unbearable, I went to Mass. The familiar smells, sounds, and language of the liturgy comforted me. But there was something deeper too. In the church, we are part of a family that will never be separated, no matter the space or the time.

Think of a time when you felt alien or other. Where was God in your life at that time? Pray for those who are lonely today.

SUMMER

August 27

'Tis the last rose of summer,
Left blooming alone;
All her lovely companions
Are faded and gone . . .

I'll not leave thee, thou lone one!
To pine on the stem;
Since the lovely are sleeping,
Go, sleep thou with them. . . .

So soon may I follow,
When friendships decay,
And from Love's shining circle
The gems drop away.
When true hearts lie withered,
And fond ones are flown,
Oh! who would inhabit
This bleak world alone?
—Thomas Moore, "The Last Rose of Summer"

The famous Irish ballad echoes the sentiment of so many melancholy Romantic-era poems about the fleeting nature of time and beauty. But its last two lines make it different and memorable. The real treasure of human life, the gift that really sustains us, is relationship. Moore's last lines are a spontaneous cry for communion.

Lord, bless me with companions who will outlast the fleeting seasons. And when even these must pass, fill me with confidence that we will meet again.

August 28

Why were you born when the snow was falling?
You should have come to the cuckoo's calling,
Or when grapes are green in the cluster,
Or, at least, when lithe swallows muster
For their far off flying
From summer dying.

Why did you die when the lambs were cropping?
You should have died at the apples' dropping,
When the grasshopper comes to trouble,
And the wheat fields are sodden stubble,
And all winds go sighing
For sweet things dying.
—Christina Rossetti, "A Dirge"

This poem is a song of death without resurrection. It shows what the Christian story looks like if Christ doesn't rise again. I imagine it on Mary's lips at the foot of the cross.

Without the Resurrection, the life of Jesus doesn't make sense. His birth in winter and death in spring are merely ironic. He should have died in late summer, when the winds of autumn are already sighing, when all sweet things are dying. Without the Resurrection, the poet's questions about the meaning of life remain unanswered, and so do ours. Without Jesus, life remains a dirge.

Lord, in late summer we prepare to say good-bye to sweet things, but only for a time. In the fallow months ahead, prepare our hearts to receive you once again.

August 29

Sometime too hot the eye of heaven shines,
And often is his gold complexion dimm'd;
And every fair from fair sometime declines,
By chance or nature's changing course untrimm'd;
But thy eternal summer shall not fade.
—William Shakespeare, Sonnet 18

"Oh, why can't you remain like this forever!" Mrs. Darling exclaims when a two-year-old Wendy brings her a flower from the garden in the opening lines of *Peter Pan.* Just this evening, holding my three-year-old son in my arms, I tried to make some lasting mental record of him now, the feel of him in my arms. I know, of course, that like Wendy, he must grow up. Change is always, inevitably happening.

Shakespeare's most famous sonnet speaks to this lament. "Shall I compare thee to a summer's day?" He tries to use verse to eternally preserve his subject's state of perfection. He ends the sonnet declaring his success: "So long as men can breathe, or eyes can see/So long lives this, and this gives life to thee." But it's a poet's boast; not even Shakespeare can stop the clock.

When I mourn the passage of time, and seek to hinder growth where I should embrace it, help me to trust that you will make all things new.

SUMMER

August 30

"[C]an it be true what's taught us in religion, that we shall
all rise again from the dead and shall live and see each
other again, all, Ilusha too?"
"Certainly we shall all rise again, certainly we shall see
each other and shall tell each other with joy and
gladness all that has happened!" Alyosha answered.
"Ah, how splendid it will be!" broke from Kolya.
"Well, now we will finish talking and go to his funeral
dinner. . . . And now we go hand in hand." "And always so,
all our lives hand in hand!"
—Fyodor Dostoevsky, *The Brothers Karamazov*

At her first communion, St. Thérèse of Lisieux was so
overcome with emotion that she burst into tears. The nuns
thought it must be for grief that her dead mother could not
be there for this rite of passage. But Thérèse said no, her
tears were tears of joy. "All heaven entered my soul when I
received Jesus," she said. "My mother came to me as well."

In the Eucharist, Jesus does not come alone—all the
souls that have united with him come with him. When we
sit with him, we are sitting with multitudes, with all the
angels and saints, with all our lost loves who've gone before
us. Why shouldn't our prayers, united with theirs, ripple
out to the whole world?

*As you sit down to your next meal, take a moment to be
especially grateful for those with you in body and those with
you in spirit.*

SUMMER

August 31

Just Home and Love! The words are small
Four little letters unto each;
And yet you will not find in all
The wide and gracious range of speech
Two more so tenderly complete:
When angels talk in Heaven above,
I'm sure they have no words more sweet
Than Home and Love.
—Robert W. Service, "Home and Love"

While on vacation, my husband accepted a job in northern Michigan. As soon as we get back to Virginia, we'll pack up our house and say good-bye to the dusty gravel of Dairy Road, the soft snorts of the horses at dusk, the crumbling barn that my children have imagined was a hundred other worlds. Good-bye to flowerbeds I never quite mastered and fireflies blinking in the dusk, and that curve in the road where I can see my husband walking home from work.

I doubt I'll see it again, unless my hunch is right and all those places we've loved, made sacred to us by our memories, are found in heaven's neighborhood.

God of heaven and earth, I make my home in you.

Autumn

Vinita Hampton Wright

A traditional American autumn is harvest time. Fields reach that perfect stage of ripeness. People work around the clock. For weeks the air is filled with dust and shouts and sounds of machinery. Then the world grows quiet, and pale skies stretch over the bare land.

Not many of us work on farms anymore, yet the distinctive feel of autumn triggers all kinds of responses within us. We don't harvest crops, but we gather memories. We don't store up grain, but we pull together our resources for the school year or work projects and store up psychologically for the winter ahead. We don't watch fields grow desolate, but we feel bareness in ourselves as we look upon our losses. We may be unaware of the mechanics and importance of dormant soil, but we enter a dormancy of our own: weeks of longer darkness in which to consider the life issues that are deep and powerful.

September 1

The ego is accustomed to keeping a tight grip on things and always having the last word. Any growth in contemplation is going to loosen the ego's grip, and the encounter with silence will for once leave it speechless.... It's best to become comfortable with the sense of always being a beginner.
—Martin Laird, *Into the Silent Land*

If I consider myself a beginner, I have no reputation to defend; everything is learning and progress. My experience has no judgment attached, only the value I want it to have.

Go through this day as if you are doing everything for the first time.

September 2

They should practice the seeking of God's presence in all things, in their conversations, their walks, in all that they see, taste, hear, understand, in all their actions, since His Divine Majesty is truly in all things by His presence, power, and essence.

—St. Ignatius of Loyola, *Letters*

Believing that God is in all things is not the same as believing that everything that happens is God's "will." Ignatius was making the point that God's presence cannot be suppressed no matter where we are or what is happening. Divine life is present to us, even in the mundane conversations and tasks of an uneventful day.

For a few days, stop once or twice to look back on the day and try to see where God was present.

September 3

Then the prophet Miriam, Aaron's sister, took a
tambourine in her hand; and all the women went out
after her with tambourines and with dancing. And
Miriam sang to them:
"Sing to the LORD, for he has triumphed gloriously;
horse and rider he has thrown into the sea."
—Exodus 15:20–21

Miriam the prophet! Miriam the musician and dancer!
What an image of freedom these verses present to us.
Miriam possessed herself and sang out what she knew to be
true. Nothing could hold her back because she had a song
to sing.

*What is my song? What do I have to say that is true
and powerful?*

September 4

[T]he Mercy is always with us; it is the ground and wellspring of our being. But unless we can connect with it, we miss the whole show—and we do not really understand the "good news" that our gospel is founded upon. It is possible to be swimming in a sea of mercy and still experience ourselves as stranded on shore. This distorted perception is what meditation is intended to fix.
—Cynthia Bourgeault, *Mystical Hope*

We work so hard and learn so much and strive continually for clarity. We grow wise as we grow old. Or so they say. It's difficult to believe that, despite all that, our perception can be distorted. Yet we distort truth all the time. We fit it to our small faith. We stretch it to match the size of our fears. Our ultimate protection against untruth is our willingness to be held by God's all-encompassing love: the mercy.

Try to say this every hour today: God's mercy is all around me.

September 5

The hand of man generally improves a landscape. The earth has been given to him, and his presence in Eden is natural; he gives life and spirit to the garden. It is only when he endeavors to rise above his true part of laborer and husbandman, when he assumes the character of creator, and piles you up hills, pumps you up a river, scatters stones . . . that he is apt to fail.

—Susan Fenimore Cooper, "A Dissolving View"

It is possible for we humans to overstep our role in this world. Where we are meant to be participants, we strive to be lords; where we are designed to be partners, we take over as bosses. Perhaps our civilization would be happier and less stressed if we stepped back from being in charge, if we learned how to exist more gently.

God of the universe, help me find my place, my best and loveliest place in your creation.

September 6

Season of mists and mellow fruitfulness,
Close bosom-friend of the maturing sun;
Conspiring with him how to load and bless
With fruit the vines that round the thatch-eves run;
To bend with apples the moss'd cottage-trees,
And fill all fruit with ripeness to the core;
. . . And still more, later flowers for the bees,
Until they think warm days will never cease
For summer has o'er-brimm'd their clammy cells.
—John Keats, "To Autumn"

Our lives, like autumn, fill up with work and blessings.
They brim over with the fruits of our labor, and also
with gifts we did not make or earn. May we celebrate this
season—the calendar season but also whatever season of
our personal chronology we have entered. May we receive
with gratitude the good things right here, right now.

Create your own poem-prayer of thanksgiving.

September 7

The only serious mistake we can make when illness comes, when anxiety threatens, when conflict disturbs our relationships with others is to conclude that God has gotten bored in looking after us and has shifted his attention to a more exciting Christian, or that God has become disgusted with our meandering obedience and decided to let us fend for ourselves for awhile, or that God has gotten too busy fulfilling prophecy in the Middle East to take time now to sort out the complicated mess we have gotten ourselves into.
—Eugene H. Peterson, *A Long Obedience in the Same Direction*

I rarely think of myself as the "exciting Christian," the one who attracts God's attention and brings down upon the earth miracles, answered prayer, or some form of enlightenment. I don't think of myself as this sort of Christian because my life is so messy and undone and at times, frankly, unattractive. Why would God give me the time of day? Why waste divine energy on this silly life?

God, deliver me from the belief that you are looking for the "special" people and that you are not concerned with frail, ordinary me.

September 8

"I've felt what it is to be forgiven. Your mistake's the same
as mine. Your hate and stupidity, same as mine. If there's
no forgiveness, what's left for anybody? We've run out of
good things by the time we're eight years old. How can
anybody start over without it? How can we get out of
bed in the morning?"
—Vinita Hampton Wright, *Grace at Bender Springs*

Forgiveness is one of life's hardest tasks, but it is also one
of the most crucial. Each one of us needs a second chance.
Then a third. Then a fourth. We need as many new starts
as it takes. We need the opportunity to try again, and
then again, and we need to grant others the space to do
the same.

*Call to mind one person to whom you need to give the space
and opportunity of forgiveness. How can you welcome that
person to another fresh start?*

September 9

We should always be wary of applying linear notions of progress to our prayer life and asking ourselves: "What stage am I in?" "How far have I progressed?" Whatever "progress" in prayer is supposed to mean, it certainly doesn't work like that.

—Martin Laird, *Into the Silent Land*

How do you measure prayer or progress in prayer? What would it look like to become "good" at prayer? What does it mean to "fail" at it? Is it possible to think of prayer, the very act, the reaching, the attempt, as itself a success? If I could pray without ever trying to judge whether I had done a good or bad job of it, would it change the way I do it? How?

Today, create a five-minute time of prayer. Do it however seems good for you. Plan what you will do and afterward reflect on your experience.

September 10

Though the fig tree does not blossom,
and no fruit is on the vines;
though the produce of the olive fails
and the fields yield no food;
though the flock is cut off from the fold
and there is no herd in the stalls,
yet I will rejoice in the LORD;
I will exult in the God of my salvation.
—Habakkuk 3:17–18

Autumn is the time for harvests. But what if there is no harvest? What if our efforts don't pay off? What if promises are broken? What if we disappoint or are disappointed?

These are the times to dig deep into our sense of the God who transcends circumstance. Because we are held in the love of God, it's possible for us to hold steady, even when the harvest is empty.

What can I do to dig deeper into my sense of God's overarching love and care?

September 11

The same wind that uproots trees
makes the grasses shine.

The lordly wind loves the weakness
and the lowness of grasses.
Never brag of being strong.
—Rumi, "The Grasses"

A friend of mine had major surgery last year and went through a long recuperation time afterward. He told me, in reference to the effects of the pain, the medications and rehab, and the changes in his emotional and mental condition: "I just feel less, somehow."

I asked him, "Can you allow yourself to be less for a while, during this time of healing?"

It is difficult to be less, to be weak, to depend on others, to feel ourselves fail or falter. Yet, we cannot avoid such times.

Finish this sentence: If I were not strong, this is what would happen: . . .

September 12

Love must learn by experience to recognize when the secret inward pressure comes from God, and when it really comes from self-will, and we persuade ourselves that it is the push of God. Nothing is more important than that we should faithfully follow our own true spiritual attraction; develop and use the talent given into our care.
—Evelyn Underhill, *The House of the Soul*

"True spiritual attraction" is a provocative idea. What would a false attraction feel like and look like? Have I ever followed what I thought was God's voice, only to discover it was something else? What have I learned about discerning true wisdom of the spirit?

Write down at least twenty things you could do with your life in the next month. Then begin eliminating ideas according to your spiritual attraction/wisdom. See what happens.

September 13

I live for those who love me,
For those who know me true,
For the Heaven that smiles above me,
And awaits my spirit too;
For the cause that lacks assistance,
For the wrong that needs resistance,
For the future in the distance,
And the good that I can do.
—George Linnaus Banks, "What I Live For"

It's not uncommon to say that I live for one thing but then to live in a way that reveals another priority entirely. During this fifth decade of my life, I am taking a hard look at where my time and resources go. I still enjoy food and security too much. I still talk more than act. Sometimes "the good that I can do" collapses into "the good I feel like doing." Lord, help me.

Write a simple statement (a poem if you like!) about what you live for.

September 14

He humbled you by letting you hunger, then by feeding
you with manna, with which neither you nor your
ancestors were acquainted, in order to make you
understand that one does not live by bread alone, but by
every word that comes from the mouth of the LORD.
—Deuteronomy 8:3

We hunger. We are built for it. We are designed to desire.
Our hungers and desires lead us to what we need. They
also lead us to the truth about ourselves.

*God, help me understand what my true hungers and desires
are, and where I might find their fulfillment.*

September 15

Joshua said to them, "Pass on before the ark of the LORD your God into the middle of the Jordan, and each of you take up a stone on his shoulder, one for each of the tribes of the Israelites, so that this may be a sign among you. When your children ask in time to come, 'What do those stones mean to you?' then you shall tell them that the waters of the Jordan were cut off in front of the ark of the covenant of the LORD. When it crossed over the Jordan, the waters of the Jordan were cut off. So these stones shall be to the Israelites a memorial for ever."
—Joshua 4:5–7

The Israelites made a memorial of stones to help them remember what had happened on their journey. We too are on a long pilgrimage. It's crucial that we remember and mark every day and every year. What are the important moments? How did we see God at work? What did we learn?

Choose your own form of memorial: a journal, photos, scrapbooks. Begin filling it today.

September 16

Now Faith . . . is the art of holding onto things your
reason once accepted, in spite of your changing
moods. For moods will change, whatever view your
reason takes. . . . Now that I am a Christian, I do have
moods in which the whole thing looks very
improbable. . . . This rebellion of your moods against your
real self is going to come anyway. . . . Unless you teach
your moods "where they get off," you can never be either
a sound Christian or even a sound atheist, but just a
creature dithering to and fro, with its beliefs really
dependent on the weather and the state of its digestion.
Consequently one must train the habit of Faith.
—C. S. Lewis, *Mere Christianity*

How does a person train her faith? Probably by sheer
practice. For me, practice involves participation in a faith
community, and also my own private forms of prayer and
attention. It's important to remember that faith must be
practiced, like a skill, or strengthened, like a muscle.

How do you practice, or train, your faith?

September 17

No man ought ever under any circumstances to think himself far away from God, not because of his sins or his weakness or anything else. If it should ever be that your great sins drive you so far off that you cannot think of yourself as being close to God, still think of him as being close to you. . . . He is always close at hand, and even if he cannot remain under your roof, still he goes no farther away than outside the door, where he stands.

—Meister Eckhart, *Counsels on Discernment*

Always, the person is the one being sought, and Divine love is the seeker. If we knew how much God desires us—our selves, our companionship, our "yes" to who we are—all fear and shame would fall away.

Consider, this hour, that the Divine longs to meet your gaze.

AUTUMN

September 18

But the LORD said to Samuel, "Do not look on his
appearance or on the height of his stature, because I
have rejected him; for the LORD does not see as mortals
see; they look on the outward appearance, but the LORD
looks on the heart."
—1 Samuel 16:7

We spend so much time and energy judging ourselves
in various ways—money, talent, possessions, looks. And
all the while God is looking deeper in at our character,
attitudes, priorities.

The autumn leaves are falling away. The trees don't
need them anymore.

How often do I judge myself by superficial criteria?

September 19

Families will not be broken. Curse and expel them, send
their children wandering, drown them in floods and fires,
and old women will make songs of all these sorrows and
sit on the porch and sing them on mild evenings.
—Marilynne Robinson, *Housekeeping*

It is our holy task to compose songs and stories from
our lives: the lovely moments and also the terrible ones.
When we turn our experience into narrative, we reveal
its sense and forward movement; we demonstrate that
everything is on a continuum. Everything is transforming
from moment to moment. We honor our pain, bliss, loss,
and accomplishment.

*Sing a song about yourself. Or tell a story. Make it shine and
reverberate. It matters.*

September 20

When anger overcomes someone, it overcomes them
with great madness, thinking neither about earthly
things nor about heavenly things while it shatters
another person who was made in God's image.
Anger attracts great torments to itself.
Avoid this sin if you want your soul to live in God. Avoid it
so you don't wound your soul seriously. Repent
while you can.
—Hildegard of Bingen, *The Book of the Rewards of Life*

I grew up in a household where much of the control was
attached to anger or the fear of anger. Later, as a young
school teacher, I discovered that I had developed the same
habits—I was controlling my students through anger as
I had been controlled. These habits are so insidious and
cause so much damage. And they don't go away easily. We
have to retrain our hearts and our minds and our ways of
doing things.

*Today, take note of every time you become angry, whether or
not you express the anger.*

September 21

Be praised, my Lord, for those who pardon for
Your love's sake
And put up with weakness and distress.
Blessed are those who will endure in peace,
For by You, Most High, they will be crowned.
—St. Francis of Assisi, "Canticle of the Creatures"

As we encounter the love of God, we are able to love
others. When we find it difficult to forgive or endure what
we don't like in people, it can help to remember how
graciously God deals with us.

*Jesus, may I pardon and "put up with" today because you
have given me the capacity to do that.*

September 22

LORD, you have been our dwelling-place
in all generations.
Before the mountains were brought forth,
or ever you had formed the earth and the world,
from everlasting to everlasting you are God.
—Psalm 90:1–2

I believe that in the core of the soul, a person can understand who she is and that she exists within the greater Soul. An old-fashioned way to put it would be to say that deep in our hearts we can know that we belong to God, not in the possessive sense, but in the essence of our nature.

We exist with God now. We existed with God before we ever understood it. We will continue to exist with God in our dwelling place. We belong. We are loved. We have a place in this universe.

Spend some time today meditating on your individual self dwelling with God. Exist in the presence of the Divine.

September 23

Again the LORD spoke to Ahaz, saying, Ask a sign of the
LORD your God; let it be deep as Sheol or high as heaven.
But Ahaz said, I will not ask, and I will not put the LORD to
the test. Then Isaiah said: "Hear then, O house of David! Is
it too little for you to weary mortals, that you weary my
God also? Therefore the LORD himself will give you a sign.
Look, the young woman is with child and shall bear a
son, and shall name him Immanuel."
—Isaiah 7:10–14

This passage makes a stunning statement: God wants us
to ask for a lot. God wants us to dream big and make
demands on grace. God waits to engage with us. Why do
we stand back from the opportunity?

*Make a request to God. Make it a big one. Ask with great
fervency that Divine love act upon your life.*

September 24

The steadfast love of the LORD never ceases,
his mercies never come to an end;
they are new every morning;
great is your faithfulness.
—Lamentations 3:22–23

The autumn is finite. There are only so many leaves on the trees, though they seem infinite at a glance.

Here is our reason to hope: God's mercies are inexhaustible. Every time you need mercy, love, strength, help—they are available, new with each day, with each situation.

What do you need right now? Call on God's mercy and ask for help.

September 25

"The eye is the lamp of the body. So, if your eye is
healthy, your whole body will be full of light; but if your
eye is unhealthy, your whole body will be full of darkness.
If then the light in you is darkness, how great is the
darkness!"
—Matthew 6:22–23

Where is my focus? On what do my eyes linger? Am I
looking at hurt and wrongdoing, at good things for which
to be grateful? Am I staring at the ideas and activities that
truly express who I am and what I believe? Or is my gaze
fractured over worries and distractions?

*God, today I will notice what my eyes are drawn to; help me
learn from this.*

September 26

"Do not think that I have come to bring peace to the
earth; I have not come to bring peace, but a sword."
—Matthew 10:34

We think of Jesus as a man of love and peace. In reality
he was a troublemaker. He kicked the pile of leaves. He
stirred things up, asked the wrong questions, pointed out
the inconvenient sins, insulted the people who could hurt
him most. It's worth asking ourselves, "How attached am
I to peacefulness, where nobody's boat gets rocked and no
one gets upset?"

What leaf piles do you need to scatter?

*Jesus, help me go into today willing to upset people if that's
what is called for.*

September 27

> We can continue to let an experience of God bear fruit
> within us by going back to it and lingering over it.
> Through this remembering, lingering, and reliving
> process, we open ourselves to God—we allow God to
> move within us, to touch our hearts again so that our
> own experiences of God ripple deep within us and can
> continue to make a difference in our lives.
> —Maureen Conroy, *The Discerning Heart*

It helps to remember that God transcends time and space.
That means that we can receive healing years after damage
has been done. Our history can be redeemed as we hold it
prayerfully and invite in grace and peace.

Choose a memory and linger on it in prayer.

September 28

We are to give ourselves over to what the Spirit is already praying within us, even below the level of our consciousness. It is immensely freeing to know that prayer is always going on, and we are to tap into that reality rather than creating the reality ourselves. In order to do so, we must simply be present to the moment.
—Frank T. Griswold, *Praying Our Days*

Isn't it liberating to know that God does all the heavy lifting? To believe that the Holy Spirit's work is ongoing, with or without our efforts? Do we trust this to be true on those days when we feel we have failed utterly, through neglect or sheer laziness?

I am always in the presence (presents?) of God

Today, Lord, show me what you are doing, so that I may participate.

September 29

One of the first things we learn in our encounter with the Lord is to stop trying to impress him. In prayer and in fellowship we begin to experience his love for us concretely; and the more we get to know him the more we find that he is prepared to love us as we are.
—Emilie Griffin, *Turning*

How would life change if I felt no need to impress anyone? What would a day feel like if I could follow God's lead and simply love myself just as I am?

I've begun to understand this freedom only as I've grown older, well into the second half of life. Finally, I realize that others' opinions really do not matter that much. Also, I understand that, all these years into my life on this planet, my basic personality has remained, and if God isn't "impressed" by now, I may as well stop trying. The truth is, there's no need to try. What a relief!

What step can I make right now to care less about what others think of me?

September 30

He put before them another parable: "The kingdom of heaven is like a mustard seed that someone took and sowed in his field; it is the smallest of all the seeds, but when it has grown it is the greatest of shrubs and becomes a tree, so that the birds of the air come and make nests in its branches."
—Matthew 13:31–32

Little things matter. They accumulate into piles at our feet. They get bigger and bigger, becoming an impressive sight. Little habits, little comments, little kindnesses, little graces. Little bits of goodness tend to grow into something bigger, powerful, and life-changing.

We don't fully understand how much the little things matter until we have arrived at midlife and realize that we have an entire history made up of the "ordinary conversations," the mindless routines, or the simple practices (prayer, journaling) that keep us grounded.

Lord, show me one small thing I can do today, or say today, or ponder today that can begin true change in my life, even if my life has advanced many decades.

October 1

Down now to the sweet bride, on
To Jesus, to the beloved—
Take heart, evening's darkling greys
To the loving, to the grieving.
A dream will break our fetters off,
And sink us forever in our Father's lap.
—Novalis, "Hymns to the Night"

As I have entered the "autumn" of my life, I have experienced increased sleeplessness, some nights when I am simply restless. In the beginning, I resisted this and became frustrated. But I have learned to use the nighttime for sitting, reading, enjoying a cup of tea, reflecting.

I appreciate the heavy lifting my dreams do, sifting through all the bits and pieces of my life. I've come to believe that there's a kind of dreaming we do when awake as well. In the groggy, dark hours, when I'm not quite alert enough to enter my usual busyness and anxious thoughts, I can sink into "our Father's lap."

Father, show me how to be present to you in the deep, quiet hours.

October 2

We may, perhaps, imagine that the creation was finished long ago. But that would be quite wrong. It continues still more magnificently, and at the highest levels of the world. And we serve to complete it, even by the humblest work of our hands. That is, ultimately, the meaning and value of our acts, Owing to the interrelation between matter, soul and Christ, we bring part of the being which he desires back to God in whatever we do.
—Pierre Teilhard de Chardin, *The Divine Milieu*

That's a hopeful thought: creation keeps happening, in my life and all around my life. I may be getting old, or sick, or disillusioned; yet the creative force keeps going and generating what is good. And God keeps inviting me to willingly participate in this process.

Today, I say a big yes to ongoing creation. Show me where and how to be part of this miraculous act.

October 3

And the Spirit immediately drove him out into the
wilderness. He was in the wilderness for forty days,
tempted by Satan; and he was with the wild beasts; and
the angels waited on him.
—Mark 1:12–13

The temptation of Jesus was God's idea. We don't like to
think of God as someone who would throw difficulties in
our direction. Yet this Gospel explicitly states that not only
did the Spirit lead Jesus to the tempter, the Spirit drove
him there. Is it possible that God drives us, sometimes, to
where we do not wish to go?

*Help me pay attention, Spirit, when I am compelled into a
situation or a season. Help me understand who is driving me
there, and if it's you, show me how to respond to the hardship.*

October 4

Imagine you see Jesus sitting close to you. In doing this you are putting your imagination at the service of your faith. Jesus isn't here in the way you are imagining him, but he certainly is here and your imagination helps to make you aware of this. Now speak to Jesus. . . . Listen to what Jesus says to you in reply . . . or what you imagine him to say.
—Anthony de Mello, *Sadhana, a Way to God*

Imaginative prayer has a long history in Christianity. One of its most well-known venues is in the *Spiritual Exercises* of St. Ignatius of Loyola, in which the person praying puts herself in the midst of Gospel stories in order to encounter Jesus. It's astonishing what can come to us when we merge imagination with prayer.

Choose a Gospel story and spend twenty minutes imagining yourself a part of it—a bystander or a key player in the scene.

October 5

Who makes these changes?
I shoot an arrow right.
It lands left.
I ride after a deer and find myself
chased by a hog.
I plot to get what I want
and end up in prison.
I dig pits to trap others
and fall in.

I should be suspicious
of what I want.
—Rumi, "Who Makes These Changes?"

Indeed, who makes these changes? I have entered the autumn of my life, and nothing has turned out the way I imagined it years ago, or even not that long ago. Who upends my best plans? Who foils my most elaborate schemes? And why does God allow this ongoing state of affairs? Maybe there's a message there somewhere?

The fact is, all those foiled plans have not ruined my life; some of them have brought me to a pretty good place.

Honestly, it's taken me this long to *begin* to understand what my deepest, truest desires are anyway.

Look at a plan that is quite important to you. If that plan did not go through, what's the worst that could happen?

October 6

Then he called the crowd again and said to them, "Listen to me, all of you, and understand: there is nothing outside a person that by going in can defile, but the things that come out are what defile."
—Mark 7:14–15

I live in a culture that is obsessed with what we put in our mouths—what we eat or drink or smoke or otherwise ingest. Of course we know about the health hazards of the substances we put into our bodies, but Jesus was getting at the spiritual implications. He was saying that our eating and drinking do not cause uncleanness in our souls, but what we actually do can defile us. This certainly speaks to personal responsibility. It also emphasizes intent and action.

Jesus, I'm not even sure I know what comes out of me that is harmful: harsh words? bouts of anger? Show me what you mean by this.

October 7

Be grateful for your talents and gifts because they are the raw material out of which you will conceive and shape your life's purpose. Whoever we are, whatever our circumstances, we can, as Archbishop Oscar Romero once put it, "do something and do it very well," whether that is raising children, teaching them to read, keeping the streets safe for them, creating dignified jobs for their parents, erecting buildings that will safely shelter them, or thinking and praying benevolent thoughts for their future.
—Chris Lowney, *Heroic Living*

Every life is its own bundle of gifts: my gifts are not only my talents and skills but also my memories, my history, my wounds, my lessons learned, my relationships, my everything. It's taken me many years to begin to accept some of these things as gifts. Sometimes I think the main project in life is learning to be grateful for what I have, not resentful for the gifts I wanted but didn't get. That's a tough lesson, and most of us don't learn it until well into the second half of life—possibly because the ego has been weakened by struggle and is flexible at last, able to rest and receive.

Take inventory of the many gifts in your life. Recognize them for the graces they are.

October 8

The tumult and the shouting dies;
The captains and the kings depart:
Still stands Thine ancient Sacrifice,
An humble and a contrite heart.
Lord God of Hosts, be with us yet,
Lest we forget—lest we forget!
—Rudyard Kipling, "Recessional"

When the wars are over and the powerful are dethroned;
when the national disasters have abated and the new
technologies have changed our lives once again; when
climates have shifted and populations with them—God of
the universe, remind us to attend well to our hearts.

*What concerns distract you from the daily work of tending
your heart?*

October 9

Mary, the Christ long slain, passed silently,
Following the children joyously astir
Under the cedrus and the olive tree,
Pausing to let their laughter float to her—
Each voice an echo of a voice more dear,
She saw a little Christ in every face.
—Agnes Lee, "Motherhood"

I am connected to Jesus in many ways, and one of them is the very human mother who loved him. Like Mary, I know heartbreak and loss, also devotion and strength. I was unable to have children of my own. It heartens me to think of Mary extending her personal borders to call all humanity her offspring, to recognize her motherhood in children from every time and place.

My own grief has turned into something beautiful as I offered my motherhood in ways other than biological birth—through mentoring, teaching, taking in a stray or two, silently blessing strangers on the bus.

Mary, look upon me as one of your children, and please comfort me in my pain today.

October 10

Jesus' passion brings us to embrace the world as it really is: full of violence and pain. We refuse to let religion and grace become an easy analgesic, buffering us from the real sufferings around us. Instead, we embrace whatever suffering comes into our lives as no longer senseless. Our suffering has a meaning in "the language of the cross" (1 Corinthians 1:18). We join the sufferings of the crucified Christ, the sufferings of humankind that he chose to embrace.
—Joseph A. Tetlow, SJ, *Making Choices in Christ*

How much time and energy have I wasted, insisting upon a life that was not my own real life but my wish for a "blessed" life? How many times have I told myself lies rather than face real pain and real violence? And how many people have I hurt because I would not acknowledge their real situations but encouraged them to deny the pain, paste smiles on their faces, and push their way through?

Jesus, impress upon me the reality of your suffering, of your very humanness, so that I can receive my own life as it truly is.

October 11

You know, Jesus, I've never been convinced that
"everything is a grace," as Bernanos says in *The Diary of a
Country Priest*. I'm just not there.
But you know that I am always here. That you can say.
Yes, that I can say.
—Nicole Gausseron, *I Am with You Always*

Most of us feel, most of the time, that we're simply not where we should be spiritually. We're always behind, always not enough, always lacking in some way.

Would God of the universe really set us up so that we always fail? Is it conceivable that what I can do and be today is exactly what God accepts and celebrates?

Lord, today, help me believe that, in your eyes, I am enough.
Help me believe that you are delighted that I exist.

October 12

The measure of [the early Jesuits'] personal greatness is
less what they found at journey's end and more the
depth of human character that carried them along the
way: their imagination, will, perseverance, courage,
resourcefulness, and willingness to bear the risk of failure.
—Chris Lowney, *Heroic Leadership*

Do you still measure your life by what you do? It seems
that in every great spiritual tradition, the real value lies
in what you are. Your character, developed by whatever
happens on your journey—that is the real treasure you're
searching for, not some grand destination or the perfect
possession or most outstanding achievement.

*Take inventory today. Make a list of your qualities and assess
what you see. Which qualities cause you happiness or
satisfaction? Which qualities are disappointing?*

October 13

When these moments happen, we could say that God has "taken root." That touch of Life will, if we allow it, penetrate down through the layers of our experience until it reaches the center. There, the transcendent God will join with the immanent God locked up, like a seed, in our hearts, and something new will grow from that union.

—Margaret Silf, *Inner Compass*

What a revolutionary concept: God is locked up in me like a seed! Do I dare believe this? Can I live as if it were true?

A truly fascinating aspect of this truth is just how many seeds I contain. Long after young adulthood and the frenetic growth and production of those years, long after a career has been established and I imagine that most of my seeds are spent—new opportunities arise, and lovely God-shoots keep sprouting.

Help me recognize that divine seed in my heart so that I can nurture and protect it.

October 14

A haze on the far horizon,
The infinite, tender sky,
The ripe, rich tint of the cornfields,
And the wild geese sailing high;
And all over upland and lowland
The charm of the goldenrod—
Some of us call it Autumn,
And others call it God.
—William Herbert Carruth, "Each in His Own Tongue"

If our eyes are open, nature will show us the Divine. If our hearts long for beauty, beauty will appear. If we place value on "God" as a way of naming reality, everything will have a certain look about it. This is the time of year to draw your sweater around you, take a deep breath, and look.

God, help me see the evidence of you that is already here.

October 15

For John the Baptist has come eating no bread and drinking no wine, and you say, "He has a demon"; the Son of Man has come eating and drinking, and you say, "Look, a glutton and a drunkard, a friend of tax-collectors and sinners!" Nevertheless, wisdom is vindicated by all her children.
—Luke 7:33–35

We are never satisfied, are we? No matter what gifts a person brings, we tend to look for the shortcomings, the scandals and secrets. Whether it's a Mother Teresa or a high-profile politician, she or he is doomed to disappoint us sooner or later.

Jesus points to the bedrock, however: wisdom. John the Baptist expressed his wisdom, and Jesus expressed wisdom in yet other ways. Wisdom has many children. Are we willing to listen?

May I be receptive to wisdom, through whatever person it speaks.

October 16

As to the experience [of spiritual awareness and fervor], thank God for it; but don't worry if you never again have it. Such things do happen to many people from time to time, and especially at the beginning of a new phase in the spiritual life, but in this life such "awareness" is never continuous and its absence certainly does not necessarily mean that we are stopping it by our own fault.

—Evelyn Underhill, *Letters*

Among the people I grew up with, certain experiences were considered spiritual and good. People used specific vocabulary to talk about spirituality. By the time I was a teenager, I felt that my spirituality could practically be measured and judged and had to meet expectations.

I had to break free from all of that during young adulthood. It was painful but necessary. One blessed evening, I realized that "spirituality" wasn't really up to me. I could receive it, participate with it, and enjoy it, but I could not manufacture it. My life of faith was resurrected then, and my later life has remained focused not on judgment but on grace.

Finish this statement: I believe that (blank) is important if my spiritual life is to have meaning and purpose.

October 17

Great love comes from bold actions and finds wisdom
for itself in all things.
Love that has discovered God's intimacy stuns the earth
with its effortless kindness.
—Mechthild of Magdeburg, *The Flowing Light of
the Godhead*

I have grown to appreciate that God's love is wild; we
cannot tame it, no matter how many definitions and
theologies we produce. The older I become, the less certain
I am of any description of God or of God's love. I say
it is bold, but it will come quietly and gently. I say it is
sweet, but it will jolt and upend my day. "Stuns the earth"
is right—this is kindness that disrupts.

*When was the last time you were stunned by kindness? How
did it happen? Who was involved? How did you respond? Or,
recall a situation in which kindness would have completely
changed the outcome.*

October 18

And taking the five loaves and the two fish, he looked up
to heaven, and blessed and broke them, and gave them
to the disciples to set before the crowd. And all ate and
were filled. What was left over was gathered up, twelve
baskets of broken pieces.
—Luke 9:16–17

Jesus began with what was at hand. He blessed it and
distributed it, as the food miraculously multiplied. And
then—this is important—there were baskets and baskets of
leftovers.

Abundance. Providence. Care for mundane daily needs.
This is where Jesus lived. He gives us permission to thrive
and minister right where we are and with the resources we
already have.

*Evaluate what resources you have at hand today. What will
you do with them?*

October 19

> If I have something I want to say that is too difficult for
> adults to swallow, then I will write it in a book for
> children. . . . Children still haven't closed themselves off
> with fear of the unknown, fear of revolution, or the
> scramble for security. They are still familiar with the
> inborn vocabulary of myth.
> —Madeleine L'Engle, *A Circle of Quiet*

What did I love when I was a child? What did I believe,
and to what did I commit myself before any adults told me
what I should commit to or what I should believe or love?
Can I remember that far back?

Unless my childhood was horrendous in some
way—and some childhoods are—I did enjoy a time,
however brief, when I trusted my child's intuition, when I
could commune quite easily with my spirit and with God.

*Find a photo of yourself when you were a child, and have a
conversation with that little girl or boy.*

October 20

Many men and women today are living, often with inner
dissatisfaction, without any faith in God at all. This is not
because they are particularly wicked or selfish or, as the
old-fashioned would say, "godless," but because they
have not found with their adult minds a God big enough
to "account for" life, big enough to "fit in with" the new
scientific age, big enough to command their highest
admiration and respect, and consequently their willing
co-operation.

—J. B. Phillips, *Your God Is Too Small*

Are you still living with a concept of God from your
childhood? Is your God big enough to fit the complicated,
mysterious world that is your life?

Write out a "description" of God, as you perceive God now.

October 21

Kairos. Real time. God's time. That time which breaks
through chronos with a shock of joy, that time we do not
recognize while we are experiencing it, but only
afterwards, because kairos has nothing to do with
chronological time. In kairos we are completely
unselfconscious and yet paradoxically far more real than
we can ever be when we are constantly checking our
watches for chronological time.
—Madeleine L'Engle, *Walking on Water*

When we are not closely held by chronological time, we are
not compelled to hurry. And because so much of our worry
has to do with deadlines of varying sorts, a disconnection
from clock watching would probably eliminate a good deal
of our worry as well. Of course, we can let go our tight
clutch of chronos time only if we trust the kairos kind
of time.

*Designate a period of chronos—maybe half a day, or an
entire day—and choose to ignore time. No watches or cell
phones, just moments. In kairos, any moment can be long or
short; its power is in its depth. And the depth is experienced
in joy, stillness, attention.*

October 22

If, then, God is real and is the One behind all things that are, we are not surprised to hear a testimony rising from the hearts of many people that he does disclose himself and the hem of his garment may be touched. And we must be clear about that—that is all that such experiences are. No experience of God is really a revealing of the whole God in all his splendor and majesty. At the best, we catch but glimpses of his nature and grace.
—George Carey, *Why I Believe in a Personal God*

The first task is to accept the true experiences of Divine encounter. Maybe I can't explain what just happened, but I know that God has somehow touched me, communicated with me. I should not discount it or diminish its importance. The second task is to refrain from judging other people against my personal experience. God may come to that other person in a completely different way and using a vocabulary different from the one with which I am comfortable.

Identify a divine encounter you have experienced. It may be a simple grace from daily life or a major event that changed your life's direction. Identify it and thank God for it.

October 23

Jesus answered him, "Very truly, I tell you, no one can see
the kingdom of God without being born from above."
—John 3:3

The phrase "born again" has been overused and misused to
the point that many people veer away from it. Jesus didn't
seem to be saying that a person must have a specific type
of experience in order to see the kingdom of God. He did
seem to say that something as fundamental as birth must
happen. The conversion, or change of heart, that must
occur would be as drastic as childbirth. God is not out to
fix us but to re-create us.

*Am I willing to go through metamorphosis if that's what it
takes to be part of Divine life in this world? Can I ask to be
more willing, more daring about my spiritual life?*

October 24

Repentance is not an emotion. It is not feeling sorry for your sins. It is a decision. It is deciding that you have been wrong in supposing that you could manage your own life and be your own god; it is deciding that you were wrong in thinking that you had, or could get, the strength, education and training to make it on your own; it is deciding that you have been told a pack of lies about yourself and your neighbors and your world.
—Eugene H. Peterson, *A Long Obedience in the Same Direction*

We often confuse feelings of guilt and shame with repentance. But what about the person who just doesn't feel guilty very often? And what about the person who feels guilty all the time?

Spiritual growth and change cannot be fastened to something so fickle and unreliable as the feeling we call guilt. How we feel is influenced by so many things. Not all of them are even grounded in reality. Some are, in fact, habit or fear or emotional upheaval.

What choice will I make today that will move me in the direction of love and of communion with God?

October 25

With wide-embracing love
Thy Spirit animates eternal years,
Pervades and broods above,
Changes, sustains, dissolves, creates, and rears.

Though earth and man were gone,
And suns and universes cease to be,
And Thou were left alone,
Every existence would exist in Thee.
—Emily Brontë, "Last Lines"

We exist in the great mind and heart of Divine love.
This love holds our molecules together. This love makes it
possible for lungs to breathe and hearts to beat. This love
joins us to eternity.

*Sit still for fifteen minutes and allow your awareness to grow:
what does it feel like to exist in this universe?*

245

October 26

Memory endowed the Hebrew people—and endows us—with a sense of rootedness, identity, and direction. To prayerfully remember is to cooperate with God in the "re-membering" of ourselves. It is to actively engage with the Spirit in uniting those fragmented areas of ourselves that have been split off and alienated through sin.
—Jacqueline Syrup Bergan and Sister Marie Schwan,
Forgiveness: A Guide for Prayer

We may try to "unite those fragmented areas of ourselves" through forgetting, or through therapy, or even through self-medication. But such uniting ultimately requires a work of depth that happens only in the spirit. Therapy and friendship and medication and a busy life all have their purposes. But is it time to pray? To open up to the Spirit sifting life, healing the hurts, uniting the fragments?

Lord, I am a little afraid of what might happen if every part of me is united—some parts I'm not so sure I want. Help me trust in the Divine wisdom that is so much greater than my own.

October 27

Let mutual love continue. Do not neglect to show
hospitality to strangers, for by doing that some have
entertained angels without knowing it. Remember those
who are in prison, as though you were in prison with
them; those who are being tortured, as though you
yourselves were being tortured.
—Hebrews 13:1–3

Hospitality is a big deal in the Christian community, just
as it was in the ancient Jewish community before it.
Nomadic people knew that showing hospitality to a
stranger could mean the difference between that person's
living or dying on the journey.

Today, we don't seem to have as stinging a sense of how
much we need others and they need us. Maybe only those
who are desperately poor or who are in prison feel acutely
the need for others' help and support.

*Forgive me, God, for thinking I'm so self-reliant and
independent. Forgive me for putting distance between myself
and other people, especially those who are difficult to be
around, whose desperation makes me a little too nervous.*

October 28

Consuming Fire! Spirit of Love! Descend within me and reproduce in me, as it were, another incarnation of the Word that I may be to Him another humanity wherein He may renew His mystery.
—Blessed Elizabeth of the Trinity, "Prayer to the Trinity"

We Christians easily forget that Jesus was never meant to be the only "incarnation"—God's life expressed through human life. Jesus was the first, leading the way for us. As the Holy Spirit lives in and through us, we have the capacity to express God's nature in our ordinary lives. Are we ready to own that possibility for ourselves?

God, make me willing for you to "reproduce in me."

October 29

> But I find that Your will knows no end in me, and when old words die out on the tongue, new melodies break forth from the heart; and where the old tracks are lost, new country is revealed with its wonders.
> —Rabindranath Tagore, *The Heart of God*

Could Tagore be saying that God's interest in us is endless and self-sustaining? Is it possible that each of us lives out the Paschal mystery of constant dying and living again?

How many times will I fall under disappointment and yet rise to another hopeful day? And when, oh when, will I forgive myself for not living up to the expectations of a much younger self? Can I trust that there really is no end to God's energy right in the midst of my life, always surging toward something new?

God, show me the new.

October 30

By this we know that we abide in him and he in us,
because he has given us of his Spirit.
—1 John 4:13

This statement might mean more to us if we were enough in touch with our interior lives to perceive the Spirit in there. We might whip up emotions in a worship service or pray with greater feeling during retreat, but if we are to know the love and presence of Christ, we cannot continue in numb distraction. If he abides in us, and we in him, and we have no sense of it, how can we benefit from that love and presence?

Quiet yourself and listen for the Spirit. Let go of the noise and activity that can prevent your sensitivity to the Spirit's movement in your life.

October 31

Let your walks now be a little more adventurous; ascend
the hills. If, about the last of October, you ascend any hill
in the outskirts of our town, and probably of yours, and
look over the forest, you may see—well, what I have
endeavored to describe. All this you surely will see, and
much more, if you are prepared to see it—if you
look for it.

—Henry David Thoreau, "Autumnal Tints"

"If you are prepared to see it." So much of our vision is
determined by our willingness, our readiness, to see. It
helps sometimes if we are startled a bit—by the clash of
autumn colors, for instance. Don't we look at trees more
closely at this time of year? Don't we notice them more?
Can we cultivate in ourselves the attentiveness to see better
all the time?

*What am I ready to see today? How have I prepared myself to
be receptive to the sights, sounds, tastes, textures, and aromas
that will fill my day?*

November 1

Our response to God's generosity is to give him the only
things God doesn't already have: our freedom, our will,
our memories, our entire selves. God has given us these
things, and he has told us we're free to do whatever we
want with them, no strings attached. Now, because we
love God and he loves us, we freely give our entire selves
back to him.

—Jim Manney, *God Finds Us*

What does it mean to give God our freedom, or our memories? What would make such giving difficult?

You would think that the older a person became, the more she would be able to give her life to God freely and without attachment. But I will continue making choices until the day I die. I can choose to let go of hurt, to forgive—or I can choose to hang on and simmer in resentment and hurt feelings. I can choose to lighten my life and become freer from possessions and positions—or I can grasp more desperately as I feel my power in this world decreasing. It may never be an easy thing to do, but what are the alternatives?

Identify one memory that needs to be in God's care, and present it, praying, "I put this in your care. Help me let go of it."

AUTUMN

November 2

What if the other transitions in our lives were also births?
What if all that pain and grief, that loss of control, that
questioning and doubting, that fear and anxious
anticipation, were also the labor pains through which
something new and special might be breaking through?
—Margaret Silf, *The Other Side of Chaos*

It's difficult to reframe loss as birth when you're in the
middle of the loss. Sometimes we can see the birth, the
"new thing," only afterward, looking back. But it's not
so difficult to look over the entirety of a lifetime so far
and see all the new things that emerged from what looked
like destruction at the time. Is it possible to see
destruction—while in the midst of it—as something
creative?

Help me look at this day, this week, as a birthing process.
What is trying to be born?

November 3

And war broke out in heaven; Michael and his angels
fought against the dragon. The dragon and his angels
fought back, but they were defeated, and there was no
longer any place for them in heaven. The great dragon
was thrown down, that ancient serpent, who is called
the Devil and Satan, the deceiver of the whole
world—he was thrown down to the earth, and his angels
were thrown down with him.
—Revelation 12:7–9

I consider warfare to be a horribly un-evolved way to solve
problems. I don't like that the tribal societies of the Old
Testament were so tied to warfare. And I don't appreciate
that great wars are presented as the final solution in
Revelation.

But "war broke out in heaven" seems more like a
profoundly symbolic and archetypal statement. Something
in the universe was rent and broken, and that is the source
of every pain and sorrow and evil we experience. And when
we are told that the war-makers get thrown down in the
end—that, too, is a huge statement to take in. The great
rent will be mended. Our tormentors will be sent away,
and everything will change.

*Today, instead of getting angry at the people who cause pain
and trouble, get angry at the evil behind it all. Get angry at
the world's broken state. And pray for healing to come soon.*

AUTUMN

November 4

If the first woman God ever made
was strong enough to turn the world
upside down, all alone
together women ought to be able to turn it
rightside up again.
—Sojourner Truth, "Ain't I a Woman?"

We women are powerful beyond what we imagine. We can detect other people's needs, name injustice, solve problems, love through horrible times, remain when it would be easier to leave, generate lovely visions, and offer courage and enthusiasm on the journey. Divine love really enjoys us!

Identify a strength in yourself and offer it to good use today.

November 5

As for heaven, I guess you've noticed, God put no
doors there.
No, God didn't. And don't you wonder why?
It's because whoever wants to enter heaven, does.
That's how God's love works.
All-merciful, standing there with His arms wide open,
God's waiting—this very moment—
To embrace us and take us into His splendid beauty and
kindness.
—Catherine of Genoa, *Purgation and Purgatory*

We are accustomed to doors that close and lock, keeping
some people in and others out. We are conditioned to
think in terms of the people who are in and who are not.
How daring to give up those categories and simply open
our arms.

How would your life change if your stance toward
others was open arms and no questions or tests?

*During your prayer for a few days, stand with your arms
wide open and see how that feels and what it does to you.*

November 6

But Peter and John answered them, "Whether it is right
in God's sight to listen to you rather than to God, you
must judge; for we cannot keep from speaking about
what we have seen and heard."
—Acts of the Apostles 4:19–20

How much harm is done to this world because people stay
silent? How many people are kept powerless because they
are denied a voice? And how many times do I bend to the
will of the atmosphere around me and refrain from saying
what I know to be true? If I have seen God's action in
the world, why would I not speak up? Who could possibly
shut me up, if I am convinced of the amazing stories
of grace?

God, make me as hardheaded and as vocal as Peter and John.

November 7

My church has but one temple,
Wide as the world is wide,
Set with a million stars,
Where a million hearts abide.
—Unknown, signed E. O. G., "My Church"

Wherever I go, I will encounter people who live by faith. The vocabulary of their belief may be different from mine, but Divine love is operating in them, and in me, in so many forms and ways. I'm never far from someone's cathedral or chapel or sacred space.

Make me sensitive, God, to hearts that follow you.

November 8

[I]t seems quite probable that God communicates to us
where we are and through the dimension of our own
emotional development. And it seems quite
characteristic of the God that I believe in that he would
send to each one of us just that sort of conversion
experience which most deeply satisfies our
emotional needs.
—Emilie Griffin, *Turning*

It can be truly amazing and delightful to hear others'
stories of spiritual awakening or conversion. But problems
arise when we start to compare our stories and set up
standards. God's dynamic work in another cannot be
quantified or judged by anyone else. Even when a group of
people chooses their own terminology for spiritual activity,
the same term will mean something specific to each
person.

*May I welcome the work you do, God, in my life, and may I
share joy with others who feel your presence, too.*

November 9

> In the beginning we are mainly taken up with the externals of our Christian life, and the Lord allows this for a time. Then, to get us and our externals out of the way so that the Lord Jesus Christ can be our All, our Father begins to take away much of what we thought we had. Here begins the long cross-centered transition from "do" to "be."
>
> —Miles J. Stanford, *The Green Letters*

What a journey between those two little words: "do" and "be." Doing is so much easier—I can keep a tally of what I've done; I can check it off the list when I'm finished. I can measure doing. But being is slippery and ambiguous and nearly impossible to pin down. Is it even possible to describe or quantify being? Should we try? Should we strive to keep track of our being?

Try to write down or draw what it means "to be."

November 10

Flower in the crannied wall,
I pluck you out of the crannies,
I hold you here, root and all, in my hand,
Little flower—but if I could understand
What you are, root and all, and all in all,
I should know what God and man is.
—Alfred Tennyson, "Fragment"

If we notice a single simple thing in this world—a flower, a wall, a puddle, a birdsong, a voice, a face—we have entered a realm of prayer. Paying attention is where it begins.

Those of us in the autumn of life may just have more time to pay attention. At the very least, we may have less energy to run in every direction and be "productive," which means that some of our evenings are free now, to notice life, to linger in one spot for more than a minute.

Choose one small thing to notice, observe, and ponder. Allow it to take you deeper into your own life and faith.

November 11

Bless those who persecute you; bless and do not curse them. Rejoice with those who rejoice, weep with those who weep. Live in harmony with one another; do not be haughty, but associate with the lowly; do not claim to be wiser than you are. Do not repay anyone evil for evil, but take thought for what is noble in the sight of all. If it is possible, so far as it depends on you, live peaceably with all.
—Romans 12:14–18

Compare this description with the average television or movie protagonist, who is very smart and proves it repeatedly, is proud of his intelligence, knows how to tell off people with vulgarity and sarcasm, takes vengeance as a matter of honor, rarely cries, and blows up everything in sight to get what he wants.

The way of Christ is different. It will rarely obtain for us the admiration of the world.

Help me apply just one of these exhortations this week, such as murmuring a blessing for anyone in my path who is obnoxious or hurtful.

AUTUMN

November 12

I know that my dreams that are still unfulfilled, and my
melodies still unstruck, are clinging to Your lute strings,
and they are not altogether lost.
—Rabindranath Tagore, *The Heart of God*

We will die unfinished; in fact, we will go through this day
without finishing something, without doing what we had
hoped, without finding what we wanted, without singing
or painting or otherwise creating what is in our hearts. No
worries; the finishing is not up to us.

*Write down one unfinished or unfulfilled aspect of your life,
and give it over to God.*

November 13

His relentless processing will discourage and baffle us if we simply want heaven when we die. But if we want what He wants, all that we are taken through, including the desert, will encourage us. Thus we will continue because we know that He ever continues to work in and through us that which He began and finished on our behalf in our Lord Jesus Christ.
—Miles J. Stanford, *The Green Letters*

Desire for heaven is a good motivator sometimes and at some stages, but it's not enough to sustain a lifetime of moving forward and growing in spiritual maturity. At some point, I simply must want God; I must want to be a spiritual grown-up; I must want to make a holy difference in this world.

Try to articulate, on paper or to a friend, what you desire and where that desire is leading you.

November 14

Now before faith came, we were imprisoned and
guarded under the law until faith would be revealed.
Therefore the law was our disciplinarian until Christ
came, so that we might be justified by faith. But now that
faith has come, we are no longer subject to a
disciplinarian, for in Christ Jesus you are all children of
God through faith.
—Galatians 3:23–26

Perhaps most institutional religion plays the part of the law, which imposes structure and information until we're mature enough to live into an adult faith. Or, maybe the "law" of religion keeps us in a safe place until we can attend in a discerning way to interior, personal faith.

Law can be too rigidly applied, and religion can be heavy-handed, but we can be grateful for the early structure and for the rules and instructions. In most cases, they build a firm place from which to take hold of faith.

*Do you hold on too firmly to structure and rules? Take steps
to embark on that ambiguous and unpredictable journey
called faith.*

November 15

I pray that, according to the riches of his glory, he may grant that you may be strengthened in your inner being with power through his Spirit, and that Christ may dwell in your hearts through faith, as you are being rooted and grounded in love.
—Ephesians 3:16–17

In the end, it's love that gives us the ground to stand on. Anger and conviction will take us only so far. Even desire and ambition have their limits. But when our roots are the love we receive and give, we have found stability that will weather many storms. I suspect it is through love that the Spirit strengthens our inner being, and it is in love that Christ makes our lives his dwelling place.

Yes, yes, I do want to be strengthened in my inner being. Please dwell in my heart and love the world through my life.

November 16

There is so much good in the worst of us,
And so much bad in the best of us,
That it ill behoves any of us
To find fault with the rest of us.
—Unknown, "Charity"

This ditty was probably meant to be funny, but let's allow that humor to inform us and to remind us of who we are and how easily we stumble. If we've lived much past the age of twenty, we have plenty of history we're not proud of, and we have proven—over and over again—the frailties in our character. A forty- or fifty-something woman who passes judgment on others is forgetting her self-awareness!

Look for the good in someone from whom you don't expect it.

November 17

Finally, beloved, whatever is true, whatever is honourable, whatever is just, whatever is pure, whatever is pleasing, whatever is commendable, if there is any excellence and if there is anything worthy of praise, think about these things.
—Philippians 4:8

Now there's a concept: choosing with real intention what I will think about. How would my day shift if I developed this sort of discipline—welcoming some thoughts while rejecting others? If I could do this successfully, on what would I focus my mind?

Today, do an inventory of your thoughts. Of course you can't note each one, but try to stop several times throughout the day and ask yourself what your thoughts have lingered on.

November 18

Christ our victim, whose beauty was disfigured and
whose body torn upon the cross; open wide your arms
to embrace our tortured world that we may not turn
away our eyes, but abandon ourselves to your
mercy. Amen.

—Janet Morley, *All Desires Known*

Faith does not give us permission to look away from
horror. It demands that we look life full in the face and
acknowledge what we see. Once we see, our hearts can be
moved. Once our hearts are moved, our minds can work
on plans of action. Once we have a plan, we can act. It
all begins with the Christ, who allowed himself to be the
victim, ever on the side of every victim.

*Christ, my example, give me the courage and the compassion
not to look away from suffering.*

November 19

And whatever you do, in word or deed, do everything in
the name of the Lord Jesus, giving thanks to God the
Father through him.
—Colossians 3:17

This instruction can seem quite limiting: I should do and
say only what I can attach to Jesus and my Christian
faith. This could be applied another way, though: There's
nothing I do or say that cannot be connected to what I
believe.

In the life of faith, there is no distinction between
sacred and secular, because Christ has brought all together
in grace and redemption.

*God, help me to see connections this week, between what I do
and who I am as your child.*

November 20

Even though sometimes I still feel some little sadness or
joy, in my soul there's a chamber where no joy, sadness,
good delight, or
happiness-over-anything-that's-got-a-name, can enter.
This is where the All Good lives in me.
—Julian of Norwich, *Revelations*

It's not unusual to feel waves of sadness and wistfulness as
autumn sweeps its way toward the shorter days, the bare
trees. As the natural world goes into dormancy, our mood
can shift toward what we see as losses. We feel time passing
and ourselves getting older.

But dear Julian points us always back to the truest, most
central thing—God's very existence within our existence.
That truth stabilizes every change or fear of change.

*Lord, I can't deny the way I cycle through moods and
circumstances. Grace me with the inner vision that stays fixed
on your love and power operating in what I do and
who I am.*

November 21

Prayer is a form of energy. It is a manifestation of the Holy Spirit, who is the minister of communion. The Holy Spirit is the source of unity between the Father and the Son and between us and the Father and the Son and all living things. To pray for others is to acknowledge and call upon this energy whose dominant characteristic is love, a love which exceeds all we might ask or imagine, a love which transcends boundaries of life and death, of sickness and health, a love that can endure all things and hope all things.
—Frank T. Griswold, *Praying Our Days*

When we pray, we are not performing a merely rational exercise, explaining to God what needs to be done. We are joining our emotions, desires, dreams, hope, and faith to the benefit of those for whom we pray. It matters that we pray. Usually we cannot see a direct cause-and-effect between a prayer and some clear result or "answer," but that's not really the main point.

Think of someone who needs prayer, and allow compassion and loving intent to well up in your heart and mind; this is a fine form of prayer.

November 22

These fears arise from not knowing ourselves. Fear distorts knowledge of self. What we really should be afraid of is obsessing over ourselves and never getting free of ourselves!
—Teresa of Ávila, *The Interior Castle*

Teresa describes what we might call spiritual freedom. When our focus shifts from self outward, the view stretches beyond a single situation and our solitary life with its worries and treasures. I'm sometimes embarrassed at how much I still worry over myself: how I'm dressed, which way my hair is flipping today, who notices or appreciates me.

Is it possible that I'm this old and still don't really know myself? Perhaps I should consider fear an indicator that I am obsessing; every time I'm afraid—of others' judgments, of my own performance—may it move me to pray, "Free me, God, please—free me from myself."

Holy Spirit, nudge me when I begin obsessing over myself today.

November 23

> I will repay you for the years
> that the swarming locust has eaten,
> the hopper, the destroyer, and the cutter,
> my great army, which I sent against you.
> —Joel 2:25

Through the prophet Joel, God tells the people of Israel that despite all that's happened to them, there will be restoration. Great damage has been done—there's no denying all that's gone wrong. But it's possible for Divine love to make up for what's happened. Imagine if we believed that grace could make up for mistakes, lost time, bad decisions, ruined relationships.

Stretch your imagination to include bad things set right. Maybe just today, and maybe just one bad thing, but imagine it.

November 24

You have been born anew, not of perishable but of
imperishable seed, through the living and enduring
word of God.
—1 Peter 1:23

After a certain age, it's difficult to think about eternity.
Increasingly you feel how finite and fragile life is. Too
many illnesses and funerals, too many wars and disasters.
Eternal life—really?

This Scripture is trying to tell us that, yes, there is that
essence planted in us like a seed, and that part of us will
endure and never die.

*Go about this day as if everything you do will have an impact
for years and years and beyond.*

November 25

Pilgrim, pilgrim, pilgrim
There is no way, there is no way, there is no way,
You make the way, you make the way, you make the way,
By walking, walking, walking.
—Ancient Peruvian saying

That's all I can do today—walk my way through it. That's all I can do with my life—create it one step at a time. My own actions, fueled by my joy, my belief, and my desire, will forge a path through this world.

Walk today with the full strength of your desire. Leave fear behind you. Embrace your life!

November 26

The wager is this: that this other way of thinking actually
exists in you, this level that knows how to sail in the fog,
see in the dark.
—Cynthia Bourgeault, *Mystical Hope*

How much confidence do I have in the Spirit who works
mightily in me? Do I believe that I in fact have the
resources to find my way through the fog and dark? Can I
recall times when the wisdom has been there, dormant and
quiet until I needed it?

Holy wisdom, teach me how to trust you.

November 27

Almighty and gracious Father, we give you thanks for the fruits of the earth in their season and for the labors of those who harvest them. Make us, we pray, faithful stewards of your great bounty, for the provision of our necessities and the relief of all who are in need, to the glory of your Name; through Jesus Christ our Lord, who lives and reigns with you and the Holy Spirit, one God, now and for ever. Amen.

—Collect for Thanksgiving Day, *Book of Common Prayer*

This is a well-rounded prayer: it acknowledges what we are thankful for, where it came from, our responsibility for what we have, and the ever-present challenge of sharing those gifts with others. Sometimes the oldest, traditional prayers are the best!

Use the basic structure of this traditional prayer to compose your own, more personal version of a thanksgiving prayer.

November 28

Evening and morning and at noon
I utter my complaint and moan,
and he will hear my voice.
—Psalm 55:17

As autumn gets colder and more bitter, the bones begin to ache. The coming of winter begins to seem inevitable.

There's a long and honored tradition of complaining to God. It's unfortunate that today we tend to get silent in our prayers just when we need to pray the most. When we are frustrated, angry, grieving, confused, impatient, we tend to turn inward to nurture our suffering rather than take it to God. Maybe when we're in a particularly bad mood, we should schedule morning, noon, and evening complaints to God. Could be interesting.

God, help me develop the courage to pray honestly.

November 29

While he was at Bethany in the house of Simon the leper,
as he sat at the table, a woman came with an alabaster
jar of very costly ointment of nard, and she broke open
the jar and poured the ointment on his head.
—Mark 14:3

There are probably deep theological meanings to this
woman's action, but I think there was another motivation,
too: she simply had run out of things to give this man
who had changed her life and shown her the way. She
had probably talked with him, followed him, helped others
come to him, even fed him and helped look after the other
disciples while they were on the road—we know that a
number of women provided for their travel.

But I believe the woman with the ointment was trying
to give to Jesus something that expressed her gratitude and
love. All she had left was this family treasure: expensive
ointment, saved up for someone's burial.

*How can I express how I feel about you, Jesus? What can I
give? What can I say? You aren't here, and I have no precious
ointment. What then?*

November 30

My belief in God . . . has kept me from harming myself.
When I really didn't want to be conscious, didn't want to
be aware, was in so much pain that I didn't want to be
awake or aware, I've thought to myself, "If you injure
yourself you're injuring the body of Christ, and Christ has
been injured enough."
—Jane Kenyon, 1993 interview with Bill Moyers

The late poet Jane Kenyon suffered from serious depression her whole life (she died of cancer). Many of us, myself included, live with that particular form of darkness. Jane's insight about the body of Christ was a revelation to me. It informs my understanding of any suffering I might go through and how I choose to respond to it.

Long-term illness of any kind can wear us down as the years go by; we bear in our minds and bodies the wounds that never quite heal. But we are part of a community that transcends individual battles and hurts—belonging to this communion of saints does not eliminate the pain but carries us with prayers, tears, and attentive love of the Other.

Remind me, Jesus, to be brave with my life, to treasure every moment I am given, and to offer it to the body of Christ as my sacrifice, burden, or triumph.

Winter

Margaret Silf

Winter. We love it, and we dread it. One person's idyll is another person's morass. It's a season of extremes, a season of paradox. Life too is a season of extremes and paradox. Our seasons on earth interweave dark and light, joy and grief, storm and sunshine.

As you dip into the reflections in this section, let winter speak its language to your heart in whatever way resonates with your own experience. Your contemplations may evoke awe at the beauty that winter can bring. At other times memories of drab rainy days or cozy fireside evenings will prevail. Some days you will want to curl up and hide from all that life is throwing at you. Others will be more expansive, urging you toward new adventures.

Every day of every season has its own unique treasures to offer. Winter is no exception. May it enfold you in its special kind of dreaming.

December 1

Besides the autumn poets sing,
A few prosaic days
A little this side of the snow
And that side of the haze.
—Emily Dickinson, "November"

The mellow days of autumn are behind us now, but the memory lingers on. As we adjust the thermostat and bring out the winter clothes, we also look out on a garden that still retains the signs of autumn, a few dead roses on the stems, a pile of russet leaves swept together along the hedge.

The migratory birds sweep overhead, but for us there is no escape to warmer climes. These days on the seasonal boundary may feel prosaic—neither one thing nor the other. But they are *liminal* space—boundary ground, sacred, potentially transformative.

How do you feel as you stand on the boundary between yesterday and tomorrow? Can you trust its sacredness?

December 2

I've been a dweller on the plains,
Have sighed when summer days were gone;
No more I'll sigh; for winter here
Hath gladsome gardens of his own.
—Dorothy Wordsworth, "Peaceful our valley, fair
and green"

As the last leaves flutter down from the trees and the straggler geese make their way toward the horizon, there is a sense of loss. It will be a long time before summer days return. Perhaps this sense of loss is for more than a summer past. Perhaps it reflects other losses in our lives—times that can never return, loved ones we may never see again.

Is there a memory that leaves you sighing?

Perhaps it's time for us, like Wordsworth, to shift our focus, to look not behind but ahead. Is it possible that we might discover "gladsome gardens" there? Today is the tomorrow we dreaded yesterday. Can we trust it to lead us forward?

*Look around you today. Where do you see the hint of a
"gladsome garden"?*

December 3

O thou whose face hath felt the Winter's wind,
Whose eye has seen the snow-clouds hung in mist,
And the black elm tops, 'mong the freezing stars,
To thee the spring will be a harvest time.
—John Keats, "O thou whose face hath felt"

I remember harvest festivals in the village where my grandmother lived. The height of the celebration was the harvest supper, with pies, peas, and pots of tea all round. Harvest supper marked the point in the year when we moved firmly toward winter. The season of growth was truly over.

It had never occurred to me that this pattern is reversed, if we learn to see winter as a time of growth. The growth that happens in winter is hidden from our sight, deep in the earth, deep in our hearts. It happens silently while the winds blow overhead. It happens invisibly beneath the winter fog or the frosty skies.

And in the light of all this, spring becomes harvest-time, when the secret growth finally reveals itself. Knowing this to be true can make the darkest months of the year into the most hope-filled.

Think everything is dormant within you? You may be going through the most amazing season of hidden growth. What is growing in you right now?

December 4

For as the rain and the snow come down from heaven,
and do not return there until they have watered
the earth,
making it bring forth and sprout,
giving seed to the sower and bread to the eater,
so shall my word be that goes out from my mouth;
it shall not return to me empty.
—Isaiah 55:10–11

I live in a place where it seems to rain almost continually, and the snow grinds everything to a halt. But I also live in a country blessed with fertile pastures, verdant woodlands, and abundant harvests.

The two go together. No rain—no green!

So what if we could see life's rain and snow in the light of the prophet's promise? The inconveniences, difficulties, and discomforts will, if we let them, nurture us for new growth, and will not leave until they have fulfilled their creative purpose. The question is: how do I cooperate with the life-giving process into which they invite me?

Journal today about the turbulent aspects of your life. Can you find hints of new growth there?

December 5

In winter I get up at night
And dress by yellow candlelight.
In summer quite the other way
I have to go to bed by day.
—Robert Louis Stevenson, "Bed in Summer"

The world turns, and so too the seasons. Thankfully the ever-recurring reversals of the seasons come upon us gently. Yet, again and again we feel the upside-down-ness of things. Perhaps we adjust our clocks, but our minds and bodies take longer to get used to the change. We shift ourselves into a different gear for the oncoming winter, but we do it gradually.

As the weeks pass, we discover that getting out of bed, dressing, and breakfasting seem so much harder in the dark mornings. It doesn't feel quite natural, and it isn't! Our animal cousins adjust their active lives according to the season while we stick rigidly to the time demands of a driven society.

Take time to make a deliberate adjustment to the darker evenings. They offer you a gift of time. How will you use it?

December 6

Nature looks dead in winter because her life is gathered
into her heart. She withers the plant down to the root
that she may grow it up again fairer and stronger. She
calls her family together within her inmost home to
prepare them for being scattered abroad upon the face
of the earth.
—Hugh Macmillan, "Rejuvenescence"

I once saw a field of violets being mown down as if it were
grass. Every single violet had her head cut off. I wanted to
tell them not to fret: the lawn mower would not destroy
their roots. They would be back.

Nature calls her family home in winter, to be
strengthened in preparation for a new scattering of seeds.
This must be just as true for us. When we feel our energies
waning, and our strength diminishing, we too are being
called back to the inmost heart of life, to be strengthened
to bring new life in new ways to the earth and her children.

Such a promise turns despair into powerful new hope.

*Are you feeling "down and out"? Picture the violets. Listen to
them. Picture their deep untouchable roots. Let your roots
speak their truth to your heart.*

December 7

Keeper of the strong rain,
Drumming on the mountain,
Lord of the small rain
That restores the earth in newness;
Keeper of the clean rain,
Hear our prayer for wholeness.
—Mary Austin, "Prayer to the Mountain Spirit,"
based on a Navajo prayer

Strong rain rearranges the landscape, gouging out chasms with its force. Small rain brings hidden new life out of what looks like a dead garden. Clean rain quenches our thirst and sustains us.

There is also the rain that falls upon our hearts and souls. It sometimes drenches us with unexpected disasters; it sometimes slowly soaks us with loss and disappointment; it sometimes refreshes us with new life where we least expected to find it.

Rain: a nuisance, a threat, or a blessing? Possibly all three? Can we, with the Navajo, receive it with reverence and allow it to grow us a little closer to wholeness?

Is it raining in your heart today? How can you allow that rain to rearrange you? To nourish you? To grow something new in you?

December 8

Love winter when the plant says nothing.
—Thomas Merton

Spring speaks in squeaks and chirps as new life burgeons. Summer hums and buzzes with the busyness of life. Autumn rustles and crackles as things begin to crumble and disintegrate. But in winter the language of life is silence.

A wise friend of mine always believed that the language of eternity will be silence. Words are simply inadequate to express what lies deepest within us. The other seasons burble with surface noise. Life goes about its work of going, growing, and dying. But in winter those tasks cease for a while so that deeper work can take place. What seems dead is most alive. What keeps silence speaks of what lies beyond expression.

Are we uncomfortable with silence? Let winter call us deeper.

Take a moment. Be still. Listen to winter's silence, in the earth and in your heart.

December 9

Winter weather. No snow goose would fly north into conditions like these. No wonder I had seen geese fighting back into the south winds, retreating from the Canadian border. The birds were waiting for spring. As soon as conditions improved, snow geese migrating up the Mississippi, Missouri, and Red River valleys would converge on the grainfields west of Winnipeg. The fields of the Portage Plains were the last major staging post on the journey from winter to breeding grounds.
—William Fiennes, *The Snow Geese*

Like the snow geese we too may hesitate on the brink of winter's threshold. No one relishes the thought of bitter winds and snowbound streets. We cling to the memory of sunnier days. We celebrate harvest festivals and thanksgivings—a last stand, perhaps, against the inexorable advance of the unavoidable.

We hesitate on other thresholds too, apprehensive of an unknown and unknowable future. We hope that conditions might improve but fear that they won't. The prize lies ahead, but only when we have taken the risk of going north of the border.

Is a boundary in your life holding you back? Let the Spirit's wisdom help you know when it's time to move on, and find the courage to take the necessary steps.

Can you name what is making you hesitate before taking an important step?

December 10

If Winter comes, can Spring be far behind?
—Percy Bysshe Shelley, "Ode to the West Wind"

Our lives change as often as the seasons. Yet it is very easy
to forget this. We tend to assume that wherever we find
ourselves in life is the whole story. We fear our toddlers
will never learn to use a knife and fork or end up still
petulant children in college. With hindsight we can see
how groundless our fears were, but at the time the
challenge seems insurmountable.

In winter, we can come to feel that dark mornings and
long nights will dominate our lives forever. So, too, with
the darkest and longest times of our lives.

*Lord, when I next feel stuck in a dark place, help me trust in
you. Help me remember that the darkness heralds the coming
of new dawn.*

December 11

Fear is like fog: it spreads everywhere and falsifies the
shape of everything.
—John O'Donohue, "Anam Cara"

Winter brings fog, shrouding our streets. Like the fog, fear
can spread itself throughout our lives, stretching tendrils
into every waking moment. Once it has settled into the
crevices of our minds and hearts, the next stage of assault
begins. Ordinary events distort into threats. Small
incidents magnify into looming shadows. You can no
longer find your way through familiar territory.

But when the sun comes out the fog disperses, a weak
and wispy thing. When we focus on the source of our
being in God, the grip of fear is challenged. When we share
our fears with a trusted friend, they are reduced to a more
manageable size. We can find our way again.

*Is fear distorting any aspect of your life right now? Can you
take your fear into the sunlight and share it with someone
you trust?*

WINTER

December 12

For everything there is a season, and a time for every
matter under heaven:
a time to be born, and a time to die;
a time to plant, and a time to pluck up what is planted.
—Ecclesiastes 3:1–2

Winter is the season for dying. Plants in the garden are
dying back, and wild creatures are withdrawing into
hibernation. As winter approaches we tidy up the garden
and uproot any recalcitrant weeds.

There are less obvious things in our lives that may also
need to be allowed to die. We might need to let go of what
has ceased to be life-giving—perhaps old assumptions and
attitudes that no longer reflect our present stage of growth.
Uprooting old habits can be painful, but this is a good time
for that sort of work.

Can we trust the wisdom of the seasons and let go what
needs to be let go?

*Is there anything that needs to "die" in your life? Where can
you prune and tidy up before the next snowfall?*

296

December 13

'Tis the year's midnight, and it is the day's,
Lucy's, who scarce seven hours herself unmasks.
—John Donne, "A Nocturnal upon St. Lucy's Day"

The feast of St. Lucy, honored mainly in Nordic countries, is a midwinter celebration, greeted by young girls carrying lighted candles.

For most of us, mid-December means short days and long dark evenings. It means going to work in the dark and returning home in the dark. It can feel like winter will never end.

There is, however, one great gift amid the prevailing gloom—the winter sunsets. A winter twilight is truly magical; the light deepens and mellows, transforming the landscape and revealing contours and depths.

St. Lucy, we learn, only shows her face for seven hours of a midwinter day, but those seven hours of daylight are crowned by a sunset glory unknown to summer's eyes. Can this be true of our own twilight years?

*Is there someone you know who is living her twilight years?
Look for the special light that her winter sunset sheds
upon the world.*

December 14

In seed time learn, in harvest teach, in winter enjoy.
—William Blake

Wintertime is downtime. Time to rest and let nature get on with all her hidden growth. Time to recognize what is asked of us and what must be left to others, and to God. We have sown the seeds and planted the bulbs and tended the new growth in spring. We have helped to bring in the harvest. Now it is time to enjoy the fruits of our labor.

In life there is seedtime and harvest and winter. We served our time in school and did our best to learn what had to be learned. We tried to teach our children and then sent them off. Now, in winter, it is time to enjoy life's gifts and to relish all that life has bestowed upon us.

Enjoy! And don't feel guilty about it!

December 15

Cold in the earth—and fifteen wild Decembers,
From those brown hills have melted into spring:
Faithful indeed is the spirit that remembers
After such years of change and suffering!
—Emily Brontë, "Remembrance"

"Those brown hills" were my childhood playground, in Emily Brontë's Yorkshire in northern England. Without even being aware of it, I watched their cold winter flanks give way to springtime green. It still took a lifetime for me to understand that what looks like death is actually the gateway to transformation.

We remember those we have loved and lost. At every communion service we remember the story of Jesus' death and transformation. Remembering is a sacred duty. To *re*-member is not simply to recall, but to "put together again," to draw together the fractured parts of our lives and stories into a larger truth, a fuller picture, from which nothing that matters is ultimately lost.

Lord, may we have the grace to remember our stories and all we have lost. Put us together again.

December 16

Sometimes our fate resembles a fruit tree in winter. Who
would think that those branches would turn green again
and blossom, but we hope it, we know it.
—Johann Wolfgang von Goethe

In the wintertime, it's easy to assume that everything is
dead or dormant. You see the bare brokenness of trees
pummeled by gale-force winds. It is hard to imagine that
in a few short months those same bare branches will burst
into blossom and hang heavy with fruit.

We know better. We have rejoiced in the blossom, year
after year, and have tasted the fruit. Even so, the desolation
of winter can erase our memories and annihilate any hope
that our lives might once again become fruitful. In the
acorn buried in the cold earth resides not just another oak
tree but potentially an entire oak forest.

*Place in your mind the image of a fruit tree at harvest time.
Smell the ripe fruit. Listen to the rustle of leaves. Watch the
sunlight trickle down through the green. Let this image
inspire you with the promise of everything you are
still becoming.*

December 17

From December to March, there are for many of us three
gardens—the garden outdoors, the garden of pots and
bowls in the house, and the garden of the mind's eye.
—Katherine S. White

I'm no gardener, indoors or out, so it consoles me to
discover that there can be a third kind of garden for
me—the garden of the imagination.

Imagination comes into its own in winter. The fire
light, the early twilight, and the long nights help us water
and feed the garden of our imagination. A former
colleague of mine, a farmer's son, was often rebuked if
his parents found him reading a book. "Haven't you got
anything to do?" they would ask. Of course, in fact, he was
feeding his inner garden in those "idle" hours. And that
garden would bear fruit in later life when he discovered his
gift for illustrating books.

Mercifully, the pressures to be doing "something useful"
seem to lessen in winter.

*What is growing in the garden of your mind's eye? How are
you nourishing it?*

December 18

The Earth reminded us of a Christmas tree ornament
hanging in the blackness of space. As we got farther and
farther away, it diminished in size. Finally it shrank to the
size of a marble, the most beautiful you can imagine.
—James Irwin, U.S. astronaut

Most of my Christmas tree ornaments come from the
Christmas markets that spring up all over Europe in
Advent. These ornaments are delicate and often lovingly
hand-painted. They are unique in their beauty, but they
are also fragile, and easily broken. I handle them very
carefully as I place them on the branches of my tree.

To read Irwin's comparison of our earth with such a
delicate ornament reminds me of how privileged we have
been to see our beautiful planet from outer space. Few
remain unmoved by the image of earthrise viewed from a
spacecraft. This jewel hanging in the black velvet sky is also
lovingly crafted, totally unique in the universe. Only in our
own times are we discovering how fragile and delicate our
planet is and how dependent it is on our careful handling.

*What one step could you take today to make it more likely
that your children's children may also inhabit this "most
beautiful marble"?*

December 19

For it is in giving that we receive.
—St. Francis of Assisi

One of my happiest Christmas Days was spent helping deliver the Christmas mail. At that time there was an extra delivery on Christmas Day. Most of the regular postal employees wanted to be home with their families, but we students were happy to put in an extra shift. So I spent Christmas morning that year delivering last-minute parcels.

I will never forget the sheer joy I experienced as children rushed to the door when I rang the bell. They would whoop with delight to be receiving an unexpected parcel on Christmas Day.

When my shift was over, I went home to my family and unwrapped my own gifts. But the best gift of all was the joy of bringing happiness to those children. It has lasted me a lifetime.

Can you remember a time when you discovered that giving is better than receiving?

December 20

O Christmas tree! O Christmas tree!
Thy leaves are so unchanging,
Not only green when summer's here
But also when it's cold and drear,
O Christmas tree, O Christmas tree,
Thy leaves are so unchanging.
—Traditional German Carol

The conifer is a symbol of resilience, a lesson in surviving a harsh season. Might the Christmas tree be an invitation to us to reflect on what qualities we also possess that are stable and unchanging, whatever the circumstances of our lives? Every cell in our bodies will die and be renewed at least every seven years, so what is it that persists? What makes us who we truly are? What lies at the core of our being? When we are in touch with that core, then no winter season can wither us.

Go deep in prayer or reflection, to the very core of your being, to encounter the unchanging God-in-you.

December 21

O little town of Bethlehem, how still we see thee lie;
Above thy deep and dreamless sleep the silent
stars go by.
Yet in thy dark streets shineth the everlasting light;
The hopes and fears of all the years are met in
thee tonight.
—Phillips Brooks

Christmas Eve, 1980. I was six months pregnant, and I had tears in my eyes as I sang this familiar carol that night. After Midnight Mass we went out into the silent fields. The sky was velvet-black and the stars shone brightly through the frosty air. Around us the world was sleeping—perhaps dreamlessly, perhaps fitfully, fretfully. Perhaps in excited anticipation of the festivities, perhaps in dread of lonely isolation.

The baby stirred within me, dancing to the music of the silent stars. For us, about-to-be parents, there were so many hopes and dreams for the life that was soon to be entrusted to our care, so many fears about the world into which that new life would be born. That night, we were Bethlehem. If the eternal light shone over Bethlehem's streets, then surely it would not fail to guide us through all that lay ahead.

Remember your own favorite Christmas carol, and let it speak its personal message to you afresh today.

December 22

Lo, how a rose e'er blooming
From tender stem hath sprung!
From Jesse's lineage coming,
As men of old have sung.
It came, a floweret bright,
Amid the cold of winter
When half spent was the night.
—Traditional German Carol

I had the privilege of being present for the birth of a grandchild. How different that experience is from the birthing of our own children. We see our child suffer, our "tender stem," the little girl whom once we cradled. Now we have to wait patiently, soothing her brow, as she struggles to bring forth her own little rose.

And then the tiny new life arrives, a fresh chapter in our family story, our own "Jesse's lineage." A bright new floweret. A new story begins. Just as we are beginning to feel the chill of advancing years, our own life's day half spent, something wholly new is given.

What happens for us personally happens for all humanity, as the Christ child is born into the depths of our wintering.

Take a few moments to reflect on your own later years. Can you see any new roses taking shape?

December 23

> When the foot of the redeemer touches the earth, the
> light within creation glows to him in response.
> Redemption is not the bringing of light to a creation that
> is essentially dark, but rather the liberating of light from
> the heart of life.
> — J. Philip Newell, *The Book of Creation*

As Christmas approached, the liturgical reading was from
Isaiah 9:2, "The people who walked in darkness have seen
a great light." However, the reader that day made an
interesting slip and said, "The people who walked in
darkness have seen a green light." This is certainly an
entertaining variant. But perhaps it is more than this.
Perhaps it is very deeply true.

To see a great light implies the drama of a supernatural
visitation—a kind of Pauline Damascus awakening. But to
see a green light is something much closer to our everyday
experience. We see green lights all the time, especially on
our roads. They invite us to proceed, to journey on.

Jesus comes among us to kindle the light that was
always there in our hearts, implanted by God, and to invite
it to shine with new vision and clarity.

*Lord, help me be aware of the green lights you give me. Help
me to keep moving toward you.*

December 24

Silence: the response to both emptiness and fullness.
—Anne Michaels, "Fugitive Pieces"

At the extremes of life's experiences we tend to respond in the same way—in silence.

Silence in devastating emptiness: when something or someone much loved is lost and we cannot express our grief in words. Silence in overflowing fullness: joy or gratitude or wonder, when words simply fall far short of what we are feeling. Emptiness and fullness are close relatives.

At the heart of winter lies the moment when the fullness of eternity—the life of God's own self—is made visible in human form. God finds expression in the cavern of an empty womb. The fullness needs the emptiness in which to make itself manifest—and all this in the silence of the night while the world sleeps.

Perhaps God needs your emptiness in which to bring something of the divine mystery to expression. Be silent with this possibility.

December 25

Great northern divers and cormorants rode a quiet sea while further north in Galway's docks gulls floated on great slabs of ice. Throughout this glacial spell the sun shone. Indeed it shone almost every autumnal day so that the seasonal lengthening of nocturnal darkness was less noticeable than in rainy weather when packed massed clouds obliterate its rays. Christmas Eve saw lighted candles in village windows, the traditional Christmas welcome for strangers.

—Sarah Poyntz, "A Burren Journal" (entry for January 1996)

It's a rare treat in Ireland when the sun shines down upon the wintry world, casting light over the ice-cold earth. But it does happen, just as sometimes when our life slips into a cold and gloomy season, we may be unexpectedly enlivened by a streak of sunlight in our souls. Perhaps a friend calls, or a stranger is kind to us, or a flash of beauty surprises us like the flight of a kingfisher.

At Christmas, however, we take on the sacred duty of kindling light in the darkness. We light our candles to welcome the stranger. We also kindle a welcoming light within our hearts, so that those who meet with us know they are blessed, with or without a candle—because Christmas is always with us.

Who has lit a candle for you recently? Who might be needing you to light a candle for them?

December 26

The seed now begins its time of gestation in the rich
dark Earth. It is the great cold of night: not the negative
images of darkness, but the dark richness of that
unknown, fertile, deep part in each of us where our
intuitive creative forces abide. The Christ energy enters
the Earth at this season. The yule log is lighted.
—Elizabeth Roberts and Elias Amidon, *Earth Prayers*

Babies grow in the darkness of the womb. Seeds and bulbs
grow in the dark earth. Bears hibernate in winter in cold
caves and dens, gestating new life. And in the beginning
the Spirit hovered over the darkness and the void, calling
forth a universe.

This darkness is a place of rich fertility. The darkness
we intuit deep in the core of our being is the vast unknown
where God is indwelling; it is the very place where eternity
is being prepared.

And so we light the Yule log, in recognition of that
much greater light, and invite the divine life to become
incarnate once more in our own lives at the year's turning.

*Lord, as the days get shorter and darker, rekindle within me
the divine life in my darkest places.*

December 27

At dusk every evening an extended flock of starlings
appears out of the northern sky and winds toward the
setting sun. It is the winter day's major event.
—Annie Dillard, *Pilgrim at Tinker Creek*

One of my great delights on a winter evening is to go to
a little market town near where I live and simply stand
still for a while in the town square. The church bells peal
out the hour and mark every quarter with their chimes.
And then, when the church clock has struck six, and dusk
is falling, the great performance begins. I could be in a
theatre, and the bell has just rung for the play to start
again, and the starlings appear out of the darkening sky
and begin their twilight ballet across the skies, swirling and
swooping toward the setting sun.

I lose all track of time during this nightly drama.
However rough the day has been, I am at peace here, and
in love with life again.

*What was the major event of your day today? For what are
you most grateful today?*

December 28

He also said, "This is what the kingdom of God is like. A man scatters seed on the land. Night and day, while he sleeps, when he is awake, the seed is sprouting and growing; how, he does not know. Of its own accord the land produces first the shoot, then the ear, then the full grain in the ear."
—Mark 4:26–28, *New Jerusalem Bible* translation

The most rapid growth of a child occurs in the hidden space of its mother's womb. The butterfly takes shape in the seemingly lifeless containment of the cocoon. An oak forest is coming to be in the buried acorn. Growth and change happen without our help. In fact, if we interfere, we may hinder the process.

The baby needs its months in the womb, simply being held and nurtured. The butterfly will die if you try to speed up its struggle to release itself from the threads of the cocoon. The acorn will not sprout if you dig it up to see how it is doing.

Winter reminds us that the mystery of life, death, and transformation is being worked out as year succeeds year, without our help, when we are asleep just as surely as when we are awake.

Think of something in your life that you feel the urge to check on. Is it something better left alone for now? Let it be. And let it be tomorrow.

December 29

This dirty puddle used to be pure snow. I walk by it with respect.
—Stanislaw Jerzy Lec

A friend of mine lived out his last months in a residential home for the care of dementia patients. His wife made a collage of photos from different periods of his life, reminding all who cared for him that he had once been a child, a student, a bridegroom, a husband, a father, an academic, an explorer of the world, a cyclist, a granddad, and a friend. She placed the collage beside his bed, and asked the nursing staff to remember, whenever they tended him, that his life was so much more than his present condition could possibly indicate.

Every time they came to his bedside, they did so with heightened affection and respect, knowing that they were only seeing a small fragment of a whole person.

Lord, help me to see that beneath the remains of every fading life is an untold story of a unique and beloved individual.

December 30

Green thoughts emerge from some deep source of
stillness which the very fact of winter has released.
—Mirabel Osler

One of the hardest lessons of the spiritual journey is to
discover that God can do more with our emptiness than
our fullness.

We put so much effort into creating fullness, just as
a potter works hard to create a jug, exercising skill and
creativity in shaping it and adorning it. But it is not the
jug itself, but the empty space inside, that makes it fit
for purpose. The hollow emptiness is where its reason for
being is to be found.

When we feel our lives are not amounting to anything,
that very sense of emptiness may be the space in which
God is creating new growth and purpose. In winter's
stillness we are invited to enter this empty space, to remain
in the still center, and to let its stillness nurse whatever is
coming to be.

*Consider the sense of emptiness there may be in your life. Let
it release its deep stillness within your heart. Stay for a
while within it.*

December 31

And still, among it all, snatches of lovely oblivion, and
snatches of renewal
odd, wintry flowers upon the withered stem, yet new,
strange flowers
Such as my life has not brought forth before, new
blossoms of me.
—D. H. Lawrence, "Shadows"

As winter sinks into deepening darkness, short days, and early dusk, time slows down. In the later seasons of our lives there is a slowing down as well. There may be periods of loneliness, as family, maybe even grandchildren, fly from the nest. There may be lapses of memory. "Senior moments," we call them.

The hope of this season is more subtle. A sharper inner vision is needed to detect those snatches of renewal when our hearts lift unexpectedly at a sudden fleeting joy. The stem is withered indeed, but what about those "odd, wintry flowers"? I have seen such flowers bloom in the life of a friend in the final months before his passing. I trust that they also lie dormant in me and will reveal themselves when time begins to pass into timelessness.

Lord, bring forth the fruit of my finest blossoms, like the finest wine.

January 1

The magical turning of the old used-up year into a fresh
new one has little to do with chronology and much to
do with the hope of new beginnings and all
that they bring.
—Caitlin Matthews, *The Celtic Spirit*

New Year's Day is a celebration of transformation. The
old, used-up year is not cast aside or discarded. It is
transformed into a fresh beginning. This renewal reminds
us that death is not extinction but transformation, not
ending but change.

Yet we resist, clinging fearfully, dreading the loss we
think is inevitable.

Yet we see in the natural world that the apparent death
of winter is where new life is gestating. In our own lives, in
hindsight, we can see that much that we thought was lost
has actually become something new.

New Year's Day invites us to trust this sacred dynamic.
As the bells ring out the old and ring in the new, what
is their message to us today, whatever the date on the
calendar?

*Is there anything in your life that feels "used up" and ready
for change? How might you transform it?*

January 2

Behold the father is his daughter's son,
The bird that built the nest is hatched therein,
The old of years an hour hath not outrun,
Eternal life to live doth now begin.
—Robert Southwell, "The Nativity of Christ"

As the year turns, from old to new, everything is turned on its head. Yesterday's endings become tomorrow's beginnings.

The birth of Jesus is pure paradox. The *eternal* reveals itself *in time*. Perfect *spirit* takes on *flesh and blood*. The source of our being becomes the one who leads us toward our destiny.

It defies all our rationalizations.

It happened two thousand years ago; it is happening here and now and always. We can't begin to understand it, and yet it penetrates our hearts deeper than mere understanding.

The one who is born will turn all our assumptions and expectations upside down, if we will allow it.

Lord, the Christ-child overturned everything. Help me to live with paradox and with the turbulent effect of your presence.

January 3

But in the final loss of everything that once was sure,
there is also the birth of something new. Where
relationships had seemed irreparably broken, an
unexpected love appears.
—Belden C. Lane, *The Solace of Fierce Landscapes*

Giving birth is one of the most traumatic experiences of letting go. The child who was cozily settled in the perfect comfort zone of the maternal womb is forced into the world. The parents, especially if this is their first child, are about to experience a shock, as their lives are overturned. Nothing will ever be the same again, for either parent or child.

New birth isn't just about babies. Loss can lead us to new beginnings. We may discover resources we never knew we had. We may find that a relationship that failed in one context can become something new and life-giving. Loss and gain walk hand in hand.

*Examine the painful parts of your life. Is something perhaps
coming to birth right now? Could this make sense of the pain
in your heart?*

January 4

Now bless thyself: thou met'st with things dying, I with
things newborn.
—William Shakespeare, *The Winter's Tale*

With every new beginning, we look back over "things
dying." We look forward to "things newborn" and we hear
those first three words, ringing out an invitation to us to
bless ourselves, and allow ourselves to be blessed.

Can we believe that God blesses all that is past? All
of the last dying year? The projects, the relationships, the
successes, the failures? Can we then turn to receive the
blessing of all that will come to birth in the year ahead and
in all our years to come?

It is a sacred moment to be present to either a birth or a
death. At the turning of the year we are present to both at
the same time. A double blessing.

*Remember any dyings or birthings that you have known,
whatever form they may have taken. Hold them in your
heart and receive God's blessing upon them.*

January 5

Surely everyone is aware of the divine pleasures which
attend a wintry fireside; candles at four o'clock, warm
hearthrugs, tea, a fair tea-maker, shutters closed, curtains
flowing in ample draperies to the floor, whilst the wind
and rain are raging audibly without.
—Thomas de Quincey, *Confessions of an English
Opium Eater*

What could be better on a winter's afternoon than to
indulge in a bit of what de Quincey describes? Imagine
the crackling fire, and the hot tea, and the flowing drapes.
Listening to the wild weather outside while you are safely
ensconced inside.

But what if you are the one who has to buy the candles,
light the fire, make the tea, close the shutters, and hem
the curtains? What if you are the "fair tea-maker" and with
no time to relax until you have made sure everyone else is
comfortable first?

One person's leisure can be another person's labor.
What might we do to adjust the balance?

*Are you feeling tired today? Carve an hour or two for yourself
from the demands of a busy day, and honor Jesus' instruction
to love yourself as you love your neighbor.*

January 6

That time of year thou mayest in me behold
When yellow leaves, or none, or few, do hang
Upon those boughs which shake against the cold,
Bare ruin'd choirs, where late the sweet birds sang.
—William Shakespeare, Sonnet 73

This is the language of grief and loss. Our own hopes and dreams, like yellowing leaves, cling to life by a slender thread, while so much has already been stripped away.

Inwardly, we also tremble against the cold of this stripping. Perhaps we have lost a loved one. Perhaps a relationship has died off and left us lonely. Perhaps we are facing the diminishment of our physical and mental powers. Where once there was sweet music and full-throated song, now the choir stalls stand empty and no birds sing.

There is no bypassing such a season in our souls. Our grief has to be lived and felt. It is a time to remember that Jesus also spent time in the tomb before he emerged into a new beginning. He is with us in ours.

"Woman, why are you weeping?" asks the risen Christ. Can you invite him into your sorrow?

January 7

*Winter is the time for comfort, for good food and
warmth, for the touch of a friendly hand and for a talk
beside the fire: it is the time for home.*
—Edith Sitwell

The busier seasons can leave us with little time to relax in
the armchair, to enjoy the glow of the log fire, to engage
in leisurely conversations, and to delight in a shared,
unhurried meal.

Now is the time for home. But what is home? Not
everyone finds "home" where it should be. Not every child
is cherished. Not every teenager is listened to. Not every
couple makes it through life together. Many long for the
touch of a friendly hand and a chance to talk. Inner
homelessness has become an epidemic of our time.

Just by listening to another's story, reaching out a hand
in friendship, just by something as simple as a smile, each
of us is able to say to another, "Come on home."

*Is there anyone near you who is longing for a taste of home?
What can you do for him or her this week?*

January 8

Once upon a time there was a piece of wood. It was not an expensive piece of wood. Far from it. Just a common block of firewood, one of those thick, solid logs that are put on the fire in winter to make cold rooms cozy and warm.

—Carlo Collodi, *The Adventures of Pinocchio*

I once had a colleague who carved wooden figures out of the most unlikely lumps of rough timber. He could walk through a lumberyard, pick up a piece of wood, and already see the new thing that lay within it. There was nothing special about the wood he chose. It was just a matter of seeing the potential that lay within it.

Sitting beside the winter fire, I often think of those ordinary logs and what could be made from them. I watch the flames leaping. I feel the fire's warmth in a cold world. I think of how our creator can see the possibilities glowing in our hearts, and, if we are willing to allow it, can turn the potential into the real.

What dream is God dreaming inside the apparent ordinariness of your life right now?

January 9

Pies mean Thanksgiving and Christmas and picnics.
—Janet Clarkson, *Pie: A Global History*

The blossom has faded. The fruits have ripened and been harvested. And now—the pie! Pies are comfort food *par excellence*. I once won a prize at school for a pie; my aunt taught me how to make sausage pie and supervised the undertaking. It was my first, and probably my last, culinary triumph.

Winter can certainly turn our hearts toward the comfort of pies. Pies give us back the fruits of the summer, gift-wrapped in a delicious crust. Perhaps every life is also like that—each with its own unique flavor, nourishing a hungry world.

Whatever kind of flavor your pie-like life brings to the world, it too will be a prize-winner, because God never makes a bad pie!

What kind of pie does your life bring to the human feast? Sweet or savory? Exotic cuisine or good plain cooking? All are welcome.

January 10

> "Has the rain a father,
> or who has begotten the drops of dew?
> From whose womb did the ice come forth
> and who has given birth to the hoar-frost of heaven?
> The waters become hard like stone,
> and the face of the deep is frozen."
> —Job 38:28–30

I remember the first guilt trip I ever went on. I was a seven-year-old. Snow had fallen, and I was thrilled the world turned white. My father rebuked me, telling me what problems the snow brought.

I knew, even then, there was a flaw in his reasoning. The snow would be there, regardless of our reactions to it. I might as well enjoy it. I wasn't responsible for the snow's arrival, but I could be a grateful recipient.

The coming of winter lies in far more powerful hands than ours. We can do nothing to hasten or prevent it. All we can change is our attitude toward it. And since the divine mystery is the source of all, we can safely trust that, despite its potential to inconvenience us, winter is a gift that is good.

Winter comes, whether we will it or not. How will you enjoy this one?

January 11

> It is no accident that the word *heart* is central to the
> word *hearth*. If we reflect for a moment about the heart
> of our home, we will have a sense of it straight
> away—whether it is lit with wood and matches or not, it
> is still the hearth place. We may know it as an actual
> physical space, but it is far more. It gathers and holds us.
> To be brought to the fire to be warmed is an ancient
> form of hospitality. Every time we come together we are
> enacting it.
> —Gunilla Norris, "Simple Ways towards the Sacred"

The Atlantic gales were raging around our Scottish home,
and the power lines were down. To keep warm we gathered
around the wood stove. For a few magical hours, the family
was gathered. Three generations undistracted by modern
technology told stories of how the day had been and what
we hoped for and dreamed of. Even the dog and the cat,
normally antagonists, lay down side by side at the hearth.

That night, the hearth drew us together, making space
for conversation and reflective silences. We shared in that
ancient form of hospitality, making each other welcome in
our hearts. The winter blasts and the lack of power were
forgotten in the firelight that bound us together. We were
truly at home.

---

*Share a friendly smile with a friend or a stranger. Be the
match that lights the fire for someone in the cold hearth of a
chilly world. Remember the hospitality of welcome.*

January 12

Bad weather always looks worse through a window.
—Tom Lehrer

Even a clear pane of glass can distort. Look out through a window on a dull day, and you may see dark clouds looming. Look through at a light drizzle, and you may see heavy raindrops accumulating. Listen to a breeze brushing against it, and your mind may hear a gale blowing. Stand at the window thinking of going out to see a friend or go to the store, and your window will murmur: "Why go now? Just look at the weather!"

Getting past that deceiving window will cost a bit of effort. However bad things appear, the reality outside will almost always be better if you go beyond the glass.

On the inside of every window is a good intention trying to get out. Open your window today.

January 13

Winter is a time of gray, velvet weather drifting towards us. . . . I look forward to the gray, quiet time for solitude, contemplation, reading, long conversations with friends. Colors are softer, sounds have more depth, the pace is gentler.
—Jennifer James

When I think of gray I think of gloom, of low clouds and cold and rain. Perhaps we get what we expect, and I need to adjust my expectations. Perhaps the presence of gray can invite us into solitude to reflect, offering time and space for a good book, a life-giving conversation. Perhaps it can open the gateway to a whole spectrum of subtle colors that we never expected to find hiding in the gray.

Everyday life can feel gray for months at a time, especially in the winter season. But what if that drab exterior holds a wealth of unknown possibilities within it? A kind word resonates gently through our day. A time of reflection draws us into deeper reaches of ourselves. A good book opens up vistas invisible in the brighter light.

What shafts of unexpected color have shone through the "gray velvet" of your day today?

January 14

> I prefer winter and fall, when you can feel the bone
> structure in the landscape—the loneliness of it—the
> dread feeling of winter. Something waits beneath it—the
> whole story doesn't show.
> —Andrew Wyeth

In the silence and solitude of a winter walk we might
well feel that we are close to the bare bones of the earth.
The adornments of the other seasons are gone: no fresh
green sprouting along the wayside, no blossom, no fruit
hanging from the boughs. The autumn foliage has been
shed and the trees are bare—their branches reaching out
toward empty skies and open horizons.

But in our solitude we sense that we are not alone.
Something waits. Something we do not understand, and
cannot see. In the loneliness there is an intimacy; the deep
of the earth connects to the deep of our souls. In the silence
there is an unspoken Word.

The busyness of growing, fruiting, and dying was not
the whole story. The deepest meaning is still unrevealed.

*Lord, let me remember that the deepest meanings are often
expressed when I say nothing at all. Help me to be still and to
be nearer to you.*

January 15

When peaceful silence lay over all, and night had run half
of her swift course, down from the heavens, from the
royal throne, leapt your all-powerful Word.
—Wisdom 18:14–15, *New Jerusalem Bible* translation

The halfway mark of anything is perhaps the hardest point.
We feel we have struggled to come so far, but the end is
still not in sight. Midwinter blues can beset us. Will the
light evenings ever return? Will we ever finish the projects
we have begun? Will it ever stop raining and snowing?

Perhaps it is no accident that the all-powerful Word
chooses this nadir in our energy levels to make the leap
from the royal throne. I think of this whenever I see a
half-moon in the night sky. There is something magical
about the moon sliced down the center. I lived in Berlin
when it was divided through the middle. The half-moon
always gave me hope that a full moon would follow.

Half-time is God's time.

*Do you feel your energy level sinking close to empty? Ask God
for the moon. You may get a few stars as well.*

January 16

The road behind us becomes what freed us up for the road ahead.
—Joan Chittister, *There Is a Season*

When the Berlin Wall was dismantled, most of it was turned into road-building material. The German people say that it was the best road-building material ever, and they are good at making roads.

In the twenty-eight years of its existence the Wall had divided families, separating parents from children and splitting a nation. It had become a symbol of human brutality and was stained with the blood of the many refugees who tried to cross it.

In its new incarnation, it became the roads by which those same people, that same nation, could move on toward a very different future.

Sometimes our roads are lined with pain and regret. But they open up a different kind of future, if we choose to travel on in hope, and trust in what lies ahead.

Lord, everything along the road I have traveled has brought me to this day, and this day is a good place to stand, and the beginning of all my tomorrows.

January 17

In the long winter nights sleep comes heavy to human
prairie dwellers, as well as to the true hibernators, and we
envy the birds their ability to forsake the northern
grasslands for warmer points south. Like the grass and
the ground squirrels, poorer people dig deep basements
to survive the winter, while the wealthy fly south with the
ducks and hawks.

—Norman Henderson, *Rediscovering the Prairies*

Nature's resilience to harsh conditions and extremes of
weather is quite amazing. Different creatures adapt in
different ways. Some dig themselves into burrows to ride
out the winter storms, while those with wings take off to
warmer climes, risking hazardous migratory journeys.

What about us? How do we react when things get
tough? Perhaps nature's wintering can teach us something.
Will we dig in and hide until the troubles have passed?
Will we try to fly away in the hope of escaping them?

Maybe wisdom invites us to do neither, and both. Not
to hide away, but to go deeper into our hearts and draw on
resources we perhaps never knew we possessed. Not to flee,
but to rise above the immediate situation, and see it from
a higher perspective.

*What difficulties or trouble do you face now? What's your
instinct? Burrow? Fly? How might you modify your way
of reacting?*

January 18

A grey
That does not ape the sea or sky,
Appear like fog or vanish like mist:
Neither pearl nor charcoal,
But the slate grey of wolves and roofs,
The slates mined with explosives,
Surfaces split and placed
To catch the beech trees' silver
And the red and green of ores
Bound in rock—the unintended,
Uninvited grace of grey.
—Brian McClorry, "A Bottle of Ink"

Winter can appear so grey, especially when the sun rarely shows and the clouds sit heavily. But the "grey" we discover here—not in winter skies but in a bottle of ink—is far from the undifferentiated greyness that oppresses our souls in the middle of a drab season.

Creation itself stalks and shimmers through this kind of greyness, the slate-grey of the wolf's pelt, the silver-grey of the beech bark, the glimmers of ores exposed in ordinary roof slates by the miners' blast. A poet's gift can make us aware of the subtle beauty in the grey of everyday, but we can nourish the art of recognizing it in our own lives through the practice of daily reflection.

Have you experienced "the unintended, uninvited grace of grey"? Will you recognize it next time it glimmers?

January 19

As winter strips the leaves from around us, so that we
may see the distant regions they formerly concealed, so
old age takes away our enjoyments only to enlarge the
prospect of the coming eternity.
—Jean Paul Richter

We can see much farther in winter, when the trees are bare,
just as on a clear dark night we can see stars that are light
years distant.

Bareness, darkness, and loss are not things we welcome,
any more than we welcome old age and the approach of
our natural life's ending. But perhaps the less our world
contains, the farther our vision can reach. In winter, we see
that "less is more." As time diminishes our enjoyments we
discover a deeper reality—the joy at the heart of things.

*Lord, may we have the grace to discover joy beyond
mere enjoyment.*

January 20

It is you who light my lamp;
the LORD, my God, lights up my darkness.
By you I can crush a troop,
and by my God I can leap over a wall.
—Psalm 18:28–29

One dark night I was walking along a country road in a remote Lakeland village in the mountains of northern England. I had a flashlight with me, but its beam was swallowed up by the night. I soon realized that I needed to focus its beam not into the dark distance, but on the few feet of road just ahead of me.

I think Yahweh's lamp is like that. I would like it to show me all that lies ahead, and reveal exactly where I should go. Instead, it illuminates only the next few steps.

And that's how I will overcome whatever struggles lie ahead—one step at a time. That's how we, together, will bring the gospel light into the waiting world, by touching one heart at a time.

Where are you experiencing anxiety? Are you looking too far ahead, hoping for a divine searchlight to reveal the way? Imagine instead the soft glow of divine love showing only the next steps you should take.

January 21

I know that whatever God does endures forever; nothing
can be added to it, nor anything taken from it.
—Ecclesiastes 3:14

The winter solstice is the zero point of the year—the point
from which nothing can be taken away and to which
nothing can be added. It is a point of stillness free of
yesterday's baggage and tomorrow's fears. Perhaps it
represents the point at which our human emptiness meets
the overwhelming completeness and totality of the divine,
where our zero meets God's infinity. It is a point of
balance, from which we can read the compass of our
hearts. The still point isn't a particular date on the
calendar, but a conscious choice to balance our own lives
around a center of stillness.

*Is there any time in your average day in which you can find a
personal center of stillness? Take advantage of it as soon
as possible.*

January 22

Honest Winter, snow-clad, and with frosted beard, I can
welcome not uncordially.
—George R. Gissing

George Gissing was from Yorkshire, where honesty and
no-frills bluntness run in the blood. No surprise he can
look winter in the eye and welcome it.

We might look joyfully on the snow and frost if we were
still fifteen years old or enjoyed skiing. But most likely we
will be complaining after a few days of inconvenience.

The cooling of a relationship, the dark clouds of
unemployment, the diminishment of health. All speak of
that which we do not welcome; and yet, like winter, they
are an inescapable part of the pattern of our lives.

Gissing's equanimity toward the coming of winter
might encourage us to accept inevitable seasons of slowing
down and cooling off, rather than squandering our energy
in a futile struggle to resist them.

*Is there a winter season in your life right now? How do you
feel about it—honestly?*

January 23

The light died in the low clouds. Falling snow drank in the dusk. Shrouded in silence, the branches wrapped me in their peace. When the boundaries were erased, once again the wonder: that I exist.
—Dag Hammarskjöld, *Markings*

Winter is likely to offer us moments when the boundaries between earth, sea, and sky seem to disappear. Hazy light fades into the horizon; the edges blur. Gentle snowfall dims the twilight. The forest wraps around us like a blanket, and if we stand still for just a few moments in perfect silence, we will know the meaning of peace.

When we surrender our sense of self to something greater, it feels that the earth and sky, the forest and the twilight know us better than we know ourselves. The truths they whisper go deeper than the messages of autonomy we have been taught. Occasionally, the boundary between the ego-self and the otherness of the mystery that holds us in being is dissolved. Then we know ourselves to be so much more than *I*.

For a few moments, stand still today in perfect silence. Listen to your heart telling you who you truly are.

January 24

Learn how to ensure that the immediate does not take
priority over the important.
—Donald Eadie, "Grain in Winter"

Some city children were taken to a farm and watched the
farmer planting seedlings. One of them asked, "When are
you going to plant the food?"

In summer the delights are immediate: we can smell the
flowers and pick the fruit. Happiness comes on demand.
Winter doesn't work so fast. In winter, the processes are
hidden and slow. The important work is never instant.

Our society expects instant results. Advertisements tell
us what we want and that we want it now. Our world
operates on a short-term horizon. Are we missing what is
most important because we don't know how to wait for it?
Is the lure of the immediate obscuring our view of what
really matters?

*How much of what you did today was in reaction to an
immediate demand made on you? How much of it was
truly important?*

January 25

Look at the stars! Look, look up at the skies!
O look at all the fire-folk sitting in the air!
—Gerard Manley Hopkins, "The Starlight Night"

On a clear winter's night, our gaze stretches for light years, to the ancient glow of far-distant galaxies. I recall such nights in Alpine snowfields, and in my hometown, as well as in the distant immensity of an Australian outback winter.

I remember a night around a fire in Chicago. As the last sparks died, the night was alive with fireflies—Hopkins might well have called them his "fire-folk." Each of us gathered around that fire was called to be a firefly, carrying the gospel spark into a world still shivering in the cold. We were charged with turning a dying ember into a living presence.

Let the starlit sky remind us that we are made of stardust, that we carry the living fire in our hearts.

You are one of God's fire-folk. Where can you help to kindle holy fire in our world today?

January 26

In places the shore of the lake rises abruptly from the water's edge. Down these steep slopes we used to coast. We would get on our toboggan, a boy would give us a shove, and off we went! Plunging in through drifts, leaping hollows, swooping down upon the lake, we would shoot across its gleaming surface to the opposite bank. What joy! What exhilarating madness! For one wild, glad moment we snapped the chain that binds us to the earth, and joining hands with the winds we felt ourselves divine!
—Helen Keller, *The Story of My Life*

This is a whoop of joy from a woman who at only nineteen months old was left deaf and blind. We can barely imagine what this joy-ride must have meant for her, and what trust it demanded, as she plunged and leapt the snowdrifts and swooped and slid across the frozen lake. Imagine, when you can see and hear nothing of the world around you, what it would have meant to be pushed out of your comfort zone into who knows what.

And yet in this hugely hazardous enterprise she discovered a degree of freedom that transcended the bonds of gravity and let her touch the divine.

Our own winter frolicking may seem tame by comparison. But let us not allow it to pass us by for fear of a fall.

When did you last let your inner child run wild?

January 27

Sharp is the night, but stars with frost alive
Leap off the rim of earth across the dome.
It is a night to make the heavens our home
More than the nest whereto apace we strive.
—George Meredith, "Winter Heavens"

Where is home? I am often asked that question, and I never quite know the answer. Perhaps there are many answers. Home is where I live, the address registered with the authorities. Home is also where the heart is, which may be with loved ones far distant.

The frosty stars give yet another answer. As they traverse the dome of heaven, they extend our vision and expand our consciousness to fill the vaults of time and space. We know that wherever our home may be on earth, we also have a home in the universe with a pull even stronger than that of the earthly home toward which our evening footsteps are hastening.

Spend some time stargazing, and let yourself connect with a larger sense of home.

WINTER

January 28

Winter is the season of waiting. It requires great trust and
a willingness to believe that this angst will not last
forever. Even though all appears dead and void of
movement, there is quiet growth taking place. During
the darkness, gestation occurs. In the caves and hidden
hollows of winter, baby bears are born. In the frozen air,
branches with terminal buds secretly grow every day. In
the unmoving soil, flower bulbs are strengthened for
their future journey upward toward the sun. In the frozen
human heart, the silent seeds of confidence are
prepared for amazing new growth.
—Joyce Rupp and Macrina Wiederkehr, *The Circle of Life*

We see the human family lurch from one crisis to the
next, making no apparent progress. We look at our
grandchildren and wonder what kind of a world they will
inherit. Will it be better or worse than this one?

At moments like these I remember the Native American
wisdom: In everything we do we hold in mind the seventh
generation. A peace activist, asked what she hoped to
achieve, responded, "We are hoping to prevent the seventh
war from now."

Important things take time to grow, and their growth
is often hidden. We must plant the seeds of the future we
long for. The harvest may lie beyond our horizon.

*What would you want to give to "the seventh generation"?
How might you plant the seeds of this gift now?*

January 29

He gives snow like wool;
he scatters frost like ashes,
He hurls down hail like crumbs—
who can stand before his cold?
He sends out his word, and melts them;
he makes his wind blow, and the waters flow.
—Psalm 147:16–18

The psalmist reminds us that everything we have is held in the power of a mystery infinitely greater than we can imagine. The snow arrives whether it is convenient or not. The frost comes down overnight, transforming our streets into ice rinks. The hail may seem like bread crumbs to God, but it can shatter our windows. The icy blasts of winter send us scurrying for warm clothes and the comforts of home. And just as surely, the power that brings all this upon us can release us with a thaw.

None of this lies within our power to control or to change. There is a certain sanity to be discovered in accepting the things we cannot change and ceasing to struggle against them. Can we hold this balance in the vicissitudes of our own lives?

Where, in your life, are you feeling the freeze right now? Can you trust the promise of the thaw?

January 30

"Hear! Hear!" screamed the jay from a neighboring tree, where I had heard a tittering for some time. "Winter has a concentrated and nutty kernel, if you know where to look for it."
—Henry David Thoreau

If we had to work as hard as the birds, we might well go hungry. I sometimes watch the birds at our bird feeder pecking away assiduously at a nut. Their patience puts me to shame. They don't waste their energy on nonessentials, as we are prone to do. They go for what they need, where they know they will find it.

Where in our lives will we find that "concentrated and nutty kernel"? What parts actually make us, and others, feel fully alive? To focus our energy on those parts is to practice discernment.

Notice those aspects of the day where you found the nutty kernel that kindled life and joy in your heart.

January 31

Snowstorms are God's way of saying, "You've been
working too hard."
—Bern Williams

Which of us didn't rejoice when a snow day was declared
and school was closed? Weather that presented our elders
with huge problems was, for us, a cause of joy, an
unexpected gift.

And now, perhaps, as we look back, we notice other
storms that released us from the daily round of work.
Sometimes it was just a passing cold. But sometimes life
may have knocked us sideways with debilitating force.

The good news is that, if we have ears to hear, these
words can be translated into, "You're working too hard. Lie
still for a while. Readjust."

*Remember any storms like this in your life? Were you working
too hard? Spend a few moments reflecting on those times.
What message should you take from that experience?*

February 1

Snowmen fall from heaven unassembled.
—Unknown

Just as the snowflakes float down upon us, so events descend upon us through the hours of an average day. Things happen, decisions are called for, conversations take place. Some things delight us, some things dismay us. Some things enrage us.

We can't control what will happen today, but we are free to choose what we do with it. Life comes "unassembled." We can make a mess of the day, or we can make something new and useful with what happens. The choice is ours.

Look back tonight before you fall asleep. What have you made of the unassembled snowflakes that fell on you today?

February 2

Winter is on my head, but eternal spring is in my heart.
—Victor Hugo

Perhaps you know people who have lived long and well. This inner quality of life often shows in their wrinkled faces and the eyes that twinkle from underneath their white hair. If you can persuade them to tell their stories, you may discover that there is a fire glowing under that wintry head that will spark a fire in your own heart.

Elders are often marginalized in our society, which is like abandoning a garden when the snow falls on it. Imagine the treasure we would lose, hidden under snow. That treasure, if we nurture it and reverence it, will bring new growth and new life to the next generation. We dismiss it at our peril.

Lord, give me the courage and the grace to allow my elders to guide me into the longest journey, from the head to the heart.

February 3

The ice was crystalline, jewelled. It held a wrenching,
violent beauty created during a time of fiery upheaval,
when seams of ruby and aquamarine were
brutally laid down.
—Joan Clark, "Latitudes of Melt"

In harsh and unpredictable climates—and the whole of
earth's climate is becoming unpredictable—farmers labor
against all the odds to wrench a living from the
unyielding soil.

Babies who smile up at us from their cribs came to birth
through the anguish of labor pains that we would rather
not remember. The butterfly struggles to break free of the
cocoon, and in doing so strengthens its delicate wings for
future flight.

I have a piece of jade from New Zealand, which was
brought to the earth's surface as a result of devastating
earthquakes. It reminds me that struggle and beauty walk
hand in hand.

*As you reflect back on any times of struggle in your life, can
you see what new birth resulted?*

February 4

Out of life comes death, and out of death, life.
Out of the young, the old,
And out of the old, the young.
Out of waking, sleep,
And out of sleep, waking.
The stream of creation and dissolution never stops.
—Heraclitus

Winter teaches us that death yields new life, which in turn will surrender to dying, as the cycle of life continues, as surely as the young grow old and the old give birth to the young, as surely as we wake from sleep, work, grow weary, and sleep again.

Now, a little late in the day, I am beginning to understand that life and death are not antagonists but partners in the great dance of life. Death is not our enemy, threatening annihilation, but an ally, promising transformation into new forms of life.

What has died in your life? Can you see what it transformed into?

February 5

Life isn't about how to survive the storms, but it's about
how to dance in the rain.
—Unknown

There is a piece of Celtic wisdom that speaks of "dancing
to the music of what happens." If this is part of what
motivates the Celtic, and especially the Irish, spirit, then it
obviously works. The Irish have survived many storms, but
somehow in the darkest hours, they have never stopped
dancing. They, along with many others of the poorest
people on our planet, in Africa, in South America, in the
Far East, have everything to teach us in the affluent West
about this kind of heart-wisdom.

Children understand instinctively. When the typhoons
come, the adults discuss flood defenses, while the children
go out into the street and dance. When the snow falls,
adults put on the snow tires, while children build
snowmen. It is all too easy to be so preoccupied with
survival that we forget how to dance.

*Did it rain in your life today? Did it drench you, or has it
left you still able to dance?*

February 6

Visitors may be hypnotized by the monochromatic
repetition of groundswells rolling toward the horizon.
They do not know the natives' thrill at seeing winter
wheat breaking through spring snowmelt, a victorious
emerald splash on the leaky soil. They cannot cherish
warm and gentle summer breezes as we do, for they
have not faced cruel, bone-stinging, subzero blasts or
black tornadic skies.
—Robyn Carmichael Eden, "Living on the Edge"

As we drove north through Montana I discovered for
myself those rolling groundswells. They had a hypnotic,
mesmerizing effect—the sheer scale of these empty
expanses, these rolling waves of nothingness. A very special
kind of beauty.

I could never have imagined this terrain breaking forth
into an emerald spring, nor had I known the terror of the
"black tornadic skies." I was seeing it all in one dimension,
without contrast, without lived experience.

Winter takes us deep into the darkness, exposes us to
black skies and gale-force winds, and as a result we learn
to cherish the gentle breezes that follow. Tenderness and
terror are dancing partners.

*Spend some time listening for the dance of tenderness and
terror going on in your own heart. Welcome it.*

February 7

It snowed and snowed, the whole world over,
Snow swept the world from end to end.
A candle burned on the table;
A candle burned.
—Boris Pasternak, *Doctor Zhivago*

I have a friend who accompanies others on their spiritual journey. She hears many stories, both of joy and anguish. When she undertakes to pray for someone or for some situation, she lights her candle and takes focused time in silence with God, holding that person or situation in her heart. She calls it "candling."

For her and those she cares for, it can be snowing and blowing and storming within them and in the world around them, but because she prays, there is a candle burning on the table, holding it all in the still point at the heart of the storm. Her candle sheds a steady light amid the turmoil. It is the light of faith.

Think through the people in your life. Who needs you to do some "candling" for them right now?

February 8

The Thames has frozen over. Birds have begun to freeze to death, particularly that small symbol of spring, the Robin Redbreast, and instead of allowing this to happen, the people of England have taken the birds into their houses so that they may shelter there until spring returns.
—Helen Humphreys, *The Frozen Thames*

The last time the Thames froze over was 1963. For a country in the temperate zone it's a big deal when a major river freezes, as if an artery of life itself has closed up.

Life has to adapt, but sudden adaptation isn't always an option. If *we* find it difficult to get by when the winter freeze sets in, what about others? What about the birds? And so the citizens take the birds into their homes, and Robin Redbreast survives another winter.

Hardship can bring out the worst or the best in us. When life is at its hardest, either we fight each other for survival or we become more interconnected with one another and with all creation. Winter calls upon us to take that relationship seriously.

Lord, what I do for the least of your creatures I do for you. Help me today to do the most I can for your creation.

February 9

*There's one good thing about snow, it makes your lawn
look as nice as your neighbor's.*
—Clyde Moore

When the snow falls, it spreads a kind of absolution over
all the unfinished work in the garden. The neighbor's
immaculate flower beds are covered over as surely as our
own unweeded borders. When the freeze descends, all are
equally inconvenienced, equally likely to break an ankle,
just as likely to face power outages and flight cancellations.
When Jack Frost visits, he paints his patterns on the
window panes of all, rich and poor alike, and like the Pied
Piper he entices all the children out to play.

Hardship reminds us of our common humanity and
draws us beyond our isolated individualism into the
challenges and the joys of community.

*What helps you to engage in authentic community? How can
you nurture it in your own neighborhood?*

February 10

The first fall of snow is not only an event, it is a magical
event. You go to bed in one kind of world and wake up
in another quite different, and if this is not enchantment
then where is it to be found?
—J. B. Priestley

Sometimes I deliberately stop, perhaps during an ordinary
walk along familiar trails, and ask myself: How would
this scene strike me if I were here on holiday? I see my
hometown through the eyes of a stranger, and I catch a
very different view.

Familiarity can render us blind to the magic that is all
around us. A small shift of perspective can take us through
the enchanted door to see the places that familiarity has
dulled.

*Try looking at your home surroundings today as if you had
just arrived in this place for the first time. Discover its magic.*

February 11

A few feathery flakes are scattered widely through the air,
and hover downward with uncertain flight, now almost
alighting on the earth, now whirled again aloft into
remote regions of the atmosphere.
—Nathaniel Hawthorne, "Snow-Flakes"

Thoughts, hopes, even prayers, flutter gently down in our calmer moments. They land uncertainly, unsure of how welcome they will be. And we, firmly grounded in all our practical concerns, turn back to our chores and get on with the relentless task of living.

And most of our dreams are whirled away again, before they ever have a chance to land and take root. Off to regions beyond our imagination. Lost forever?

A few of those feathery flakes settle on the restless landscapes of our hearts. A few begin to grow. Not all are lost. Some of our fragile dreams take root and grow strong, and bear fruit for the world. Let us not grieve for those that flew away, but rather nourish those that stayed.

Which of your heart's dreams have settled and taken root?
How might you nourish them even more?

February 12

And when old Winter puts his blank face to the glass,
I shall close all my shutters, pull the curtains tight,
and build me stately palaces by candlelight.
—Charles Baudelaire, "Landscape"

In winter days when I was a child, my breath would freeze on the window pane. A blank face gazed back at me. The frost on the glass obscured anything I might see beyond. I would close the curtains firmly and move as close as possible to the fireside.

Sometimes, the world beyond us seems a blank unknown, and we withdraw into the safety of imagination, which is powerful, but also a two-edged sword. It consoles us and inspires, but it also magnifies and pulls us into a destructive spiral. Sometimes it is good to withdraw and reflect. Sometimes we need to push beyond the blankness.

When the world presents you with a blank face, what kind of picture does your imagination tend to create: one to inspire you or one to close you down?

February 13

Everything was sparkled and sharp as if the world were
new, hatched that very morning from an icy egg. Willow
branches were cloaked in hoar frost, waterfalls encased
in ice, and the snowy land speckled with the tracks of a
hundred wild animals: red-backed voles, coyotes and fox,
fat-footed lynx, moose and dancing magpies.
—Eowyn Ivey, "The Snow Child"

Winter morning: the first visitor to the frozen landscape
is the sunlight, setting everything a-sparkle. A whole new
world, it seems, has come from nowhere, descended
overnight, "hatched from an icy egg."

And then we discover that the sheet is not blank at
all, but criss-crossed by the tracks of wild creatures. We
rarely see them, but we know they are there, the mystery of
otherness walking among us, unseen.

*Where have you caught glimpses of the divine mystery
today—footprints of the sacred, criss-crossing your ordinary
daily living? Did anything in today's experience make you
catch your breath in wonder?*

February 14

The hail flew in showers. I heard naught there save the
sea booming, the ice-cold billow, at times the song of
the swan. I took my gladness in the cry of the gannet
and the sound of the curlew instead of the laughter of
men, in the screaming of gull instead of the
drink of mead.
—Anonymous, "The Seafarer"

I see this ancient seafarer standing on the shores of these
northern islands, observing the inexorable advance of a
harsh and unforgiving winter: showers of hail stinging like
needles, a thunderous ocean swell, and everywhere the
biting cold, seeping into the very marrow of his bones.

And yet the final word isn't one of grim submission,
but an expression of joy. There will be no human company
here to gladden his heart, no mead to warm his solitary
days, but he can nevertheless rejoice in the gannet's cry and
the sound of the curlew.

That takes a special kind of stoicism. And what of
ourselves? When life is harsh, do we focus on the hardships
or on the glimmers of joy that shine through the gloom?

Lord, may I have the grace to enjoy what I am doing.

February 15

For the unlearned, old age is winter; for the learned it is
the season of harvest.
—The Talmud

Could the winter season of our life actually be the richest
season of all, when the harvest is gathered in and shared?
To be a winter harvester might be to share our wisdom
with future generations and offer a wider, longer
perspective on the difficulties they face.

Socrates said, "The unexamined life is not worth
living." In our winter season we are invited to reflect on
our years, and bring forth the crop of wisdom that is ours
alone to yield.

*Have you thought of writing down, or recording, your
memories and reflections for the young people in your family?*

February 16

There is simply the rose; it is perfect in every moment of
its existence. Before a leaf-bud has burst, its whole life
acts; in the full-blown flower there is no more; in the
leafless root there is no less.
—Ralph Waldo Emerson, "Self-Reliance"

To see the whole is a gift given only to the wisest. Can we
also look at our lives and let go of the hierarchy of value we
tend to place on each of its parts?

The full flower would usually get first place in that
hierarchy—when we are at the peak of our energy and
achievement. The new bud would probably come second,
with all its hidden promise. But the leafless root would
come nowhere at all in the scheme of things. It lies in
our hearts, ignored and overlooked as we wait for our days
to end.

And yet that very same leafless root contains all our
tomorrows—both temporal and eternal. Down there in
the dark earth it holds the future. Every stage of life is the
whole, no more, no less.

*Remember: there is simply you, perfect in every stage of your
being, loved and cherished in your completeness by the Love
that created you. Pray your gratitude.*

February 17

> O Winter! Ruler of the inverted year . . .
> I crown thee King of intimate delights,
> fireside enjoyments, home-born happiness.
> And all the comforts that the lowly roof
> of undisturb'd retirement and the hours,
> and of long uninterrupted evening, knows.
> —William Cowper, "The Task"

In these northern latitudes I can read a newspaper outside at midnight in June. In December night falls at four o'clock in the afternoon. The year has indeed turned upside down. This inversion challenges us to adapt to a completely different daily routine. The changing season brings changing tasks and duties, and also invites us to relax in different ways.

The coals of the barbecue give way to the logs in the hearth. The hiking trails lead us gently back to home. What might that mean for us today, when all too often the evenings pass in the thrall of the Internet or television?

For me, one of heaven's mansions would definitely be a place to curl up with a good book, and immerse myself, undisturbed, in the world of the imagination. Winter gives me glimpses of this mansion.

What does "home-born happiness" mean for you, and how might you engage in it more fully, either alone or with family and friends?

February 18

Keen, fitful gusts are whisp'ring here and there
Among the bushes half leafless and dry;
The stars look very cold about the sky,
And I have many miles on foot to fare.
—John Keats, Sonnet IX

We have a little flock of goldfinches who frequent our bird feeder. For them the search for food in winter is a daily struggle. The temperature is dropping, and a whole long winter stretches out ahead. There are many hard miles to go before spring returns to restock nature's larder.

There are days when we too look ahead and see the long march of months and years that we still have to walk. We don't know how we will keep going. But somewhere along the way there will be unexpected resources: an encouraging conversation, a gathering with friends, a visit from our children—"bird feeders" offering kindness to sustain the journey.

Who, or what, feeds your soul when times are hard? How might you be a source of sustenance for others?

February 19

The winter is kind and leaves red berries on the boughs
for hungry sparrows.
—John Geddes, "A Familiar Rain"

Winter is harsh. Winter is cold. Winter means hunger, especially for the garden birds and wild creatures. Winter is about survival, and survival can be tough.

But John Geddes sees a different quality in the winter landscape. Not the frost but the berries. Not a ruthless, relentless force working against us, but a compassionate generosity that sets out a tasty morsel for the struggling sparrows.

It's simply a matter of perspective. The difference lies in the eye of the beholder. How do we view the harsher aspects of our own lives? Do we see the struggle first, or the gifts? Can we see the berries through the frost?

Take a closer look at any hard situation in your life right now. Are there any berries on the boughs that you may not have noticed?

February 20

*A snowflake is one of God's most fragile creations, but
look what they can do when they stick together.*
—Author Unknown

Humans are fragile. We can be forging ahead full steam
one minute, and lying in the emergency room the next;
CEO of a major corporation one day, and unemployed
the next; in love one moment, and devastated by
disappointment the next. We break easily.

Snowflakes are even more fragile. A few degrees of
warmth and they dissolve into nothing. But when they
stick together they can bring our lives to a grinding halt
and transform our world into an enchanted landscape.
They can cause us to huddle round the fire or draw us out
to play.

Individually we may feel helpless. But when we stick
together . . . ?

*Help me to remember, Lord, that alone I can do very little.
Together there is very little we cannot do.*

February 21

Spiders evidently as surprised by the weather as the rest
of us: their webs were still everywhere—little silken
laundry lines with perfect snowflakes hung out in
rows to dry.
—Leslie Land, *The 3,000 Mile Garden*

Have you ever walked along a grimy urban street, when
the first frosts have visited overnight, and perhaps the first
snowflakes have fallen, and been bewitched by the sight of
the most perfect lace-making displays on the bushes and
walls and even on the dumpsters?

It takes the mind of a child—or a child of God!—to
think of these works of art as little laundry lines, where the
snowflakes hang out to dry. The morning sun sets these
silky masterpieces ablaze with undeniable glory.

*Watch out today for some little detail of nature's handiwork
that makes you catch your breath in wonder.*

February 22

We are each at any given moment facing the doorway of
our own magical cabin, if not already in it. This cabin is
not somewhere else. It stands before us right here, right
now. If we listen closely, we can hear a still, small voice
deep inside. Its stillness invites us in, and its smallness lets
us know that we have arrived home.
—Michael Gellert, "The Way of the Small"

One day, while skiing in the high Alpine peaks, I was
caught with some friends, lost in a blinding blizzard. And
then, as if heaven-sent, we came upon a mountain cabin.
Inside a group of stranded skiers welcomed us warmly. We
spent the day with them, sharing stories and songs until we
were ready to tackle the descent together.

Sometimes we only need to go through the door,
following the call of the still small voice in our hearts.
There we will find ourselves, and each other.

*Take time to go to your magical cabin today and listen to the
stillness within you. No need to wait for the blizzard before
you seek it out.*

February 23

Adversity draws men together and produces beauty and
harmony in life's relationships, just as the cold of winter
produces ice-flowers on the window-panes, which
vanish with the warmth.
—Søren Kierkegaard

Neighbors we barely know in good weather become
neighbors in need when the snow falls or the floods rise.
Beautiful bonds can be formed in such circumstances, as
we reach out to help each other, bonds as beautiful as ice
flowers produced on window panes by fleeting frosts.

How sad, if these human ice flowers are allowed to melt
away when the sun shines again, and our mutual concerns
and caring are forgotten in the warmth of easier times.

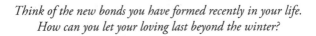

Think of the new bonds you have formed recently in your life.
How can you let your loving last beyond the winter?

February 24

Imagine the solitary sled-track running far up into the
snowy and evergreen wilderness, hemmed in closely for
a hundred miles by the forest, and again stretching
straight across the broad surfaces of concealed lakes!
—Henry David Thoreau, *The Maine Woods*

We are like a solitary sled in a winter landscape, weaving
through the constantly unfolding terrain of life. Perhaps
the trail begins in familiar territory, where there is bustle
and activity and the chatter of other people. But the winter
seasons of life can take us to more solitary inner pathways,
sometimes through dense conifer forests where there is
almost no light along the path, sometimes traversing
frozen lakes where the sunlight dazzles us in its glittering
reflection. The trail can even lead us beyond the tree line
where we face both challenge and beauty.

*How does the sled trail of your life look? Try describing it to
yourself, in pictures or in words.*

February 25

One kind word can warm three winter months.
—Japanese proverb

There is weather-warmth. And there is heart-warmth. This Japanese wisdom suggests that heart-warmth is able to transform the coldest weather. The chillier a person's life circumstances are, the more powerful one kind word can be, spreading through the person like a warm glow.

So, for someone who rarely sees another living soul from one week's end to the next, a friendly word from someone who actually cares can make an enormous difference. For the elderly shut-in, a visit from a friend or relative can change dismal loneliness into unexpected joy.

One kind word is in everyone's vocabulary.

Is there anything you can do or say to warm up someone's life today?

February 26

"If we wrapped up against the cold, we wouldn't feel the other things, like the bright tingle of the stars or the music of the Aurora, or best of all the silky feeling of moonlight on our skin. It's worth being cold for that."
—Philip Pullman, *The Golden Compass*

I cherish many memories of moments of wonder accompanied by hours of discomfort: a night beneath the southern stars, when our shelter was a very basic miner's hut; a chance to explore the canyons and forests of North America sleeping in only a tent; the glimpse of a golden eagle at the end of an arduous mountain scramble; a Scottish mountain peak arrived at through an ambush of mosquitoes; the laughter and companionship of a mountain hut while a blizzard swirled all around.

I would never trade these memories for an easier life.

Sift through your memories. What hard times do you now cherish?

February 27

In the depth of winter, I finally learned that within me there lay an invincible summer.
—Albert Camus

I had an e-mail from a friend in Canada the other day. Her home had been devastated by floods, her possessions strewn around the backyard.

But in the midst of the mayhem, their little bird house was still intact, a wren sitting on top of it, singing her heart out. The joy of the wren, my friend tells me, far outweighs her own sorrow at the sudden loss of so much that she held dear.

Sometimes we only discover what really matters when all the outer wrappings are torn away. The times when our lives seem to fall apart may be the points when we catch sight of a burning in the core of our being—a light that the darkness cannot extinguish.

In the worst experiences of your life, have you ever caught a glimpse of the best that you can be?

February 28

No snowflake ever falls in the wrong place.
—Zen proverb

Every snowflake carries the potential to cause us to slip and break a bone, or to subvert our travel plans or ground us where we don't want to be grounded. So is this Zen wisdom true?

Perhaps we can't always see it, and perhaps we never will, but often enough, when we look back, we can glimpse the truth of it. Whatever happens, however unwelcome, has usually brought some blessing with it, even though that blessing may have been wrapped in thorns and taken us a long time to unpack.

Have any of the unwanted and potentially harmful events in your life also brought blessing and beauty?

February 29

> "You have survived the winter because you are, and
> were, and always will be very much loved," said the sun.
> "For that small place deep within you that remained
> unfrozen and open to mystery, that is where I have made
> my dwelling."
> —Mary Fahy, *The Tree That Survived the Winter*

You are alive today! You are a survivor! You may have lived
through the worst! Your inner journey, too, may have come
close to derailment, through doubt or disillusionment or a
sense of betrayal. But you are still here, not just alive but
actively seeking to grow and become more fully the person
you can be.

What has carried you through all the crises and
disasters, all the inner turmoil and upheaval?

The tree in this story survives because there is a deep
center at its heart that is always open to mystery. Let us
nourish the molten core of love within each of us and
remain always open to its mystery.

Look at your reflection in the mirror. What do you see?

About the Authors

Ginny Kubitz Moyer is a contributor to several print and online publications, including *U.S. Catholic* magazine, BustedHalo.com, and CatholicMom.com. Her book *Mary and Me* is a Catholic Press Award winner. Moyer's most recent book is *Random MOMents of Grace*, and she blogs at RandomActsOfMomness.com. She lives in the San Francisco Bay area with her husband and two sons.

Jessica Mesman Griffith is the author, with Amy Andrews, of *Love and Salt: A Spiritual Friendship Shared in Letters*, and a regular contributor to Good Letters: The *Image* Blog. She lives in northern Michigan with her husband, writer David Griffith, and children.

Vinita Hampton Wright is a Loyola Press editor and writer of many books, including *Days of Deepening Friendship*, *Simple Acts of Moving Forward*, and most recently, *The Art of Spiritual Writing*. She blogs for DeepeningFriendship.com and lives in Chicago, Illinois, with her husband, dog, and two cats.

Margaret Silf travels widely in her work as a retreat director and speaker on Ignatian spirituality. Her books include *Close to the Heart: A Guide to Personal Prayer*, *The Other Side of Chaos*, *Inner Compass*, and most recently, *Just Call Me López*.